D1590923

ASPECTS OF VIETNAMESE HISTORY

ASIAN STUDIES AT HAWAII

The Publications Committee of the Asian Studies Program will consider all manuscripts for inclusion in the series, but primary consideration will be given to the research results of graduate students and faculty at the University of Hawaii. The series includes monographs, occasional papers, translations with commentaries, and research aids.

Orders for back issues and future issues should be directed to The University Press of Hawaii, 535 Ward Avenue, Honolulu, Hawaii 96814, USA. Present standing orders will continue to be filled without special notification.

Asian Studies at Hawaii, No. 8

ASPECTS OF VIETNAMESE HISTORY

Edited

by

Walter F. Vella

Asian Studies Program
University of Hawaii

The University Press of Hawaii
1973

This volume, the eighth in the series entitled *Asian Studies at Hawaii,* is the fourth to concern Southeast Asia. A complete list of all titles in the series may be found at the end of this volume.

Southeast Asian Studies at the University of Hawaii is administratively part of the Asian Studies Program. The Program offers interdisciplinary majors in Asian studies at both the undergraduate and M.A. levels. The program also facilitates research, organizes lecture programs, sponsors publications, and launches other efforts at broadening understanding of Asia.

Further information about faculty and staff, degree requirements, course offerings, and other resources of Southeast Asian Studies may be obtained by writing Southeast Asian Studies, Asian Studies Program, 315 Moore Hall, University of Hawaii, Honolulu, Hawaii 96822.

Library of Congress Catalog Card Number 72-619626
ISBN 0-8248-0236-5
Copyright © 1973 by The University Press
    of Hawaii
All rights reserved
Manufactured in the United States of America

CONTENTS

PREFACE

Here is a potpourri of papers on Vietnam. They
are by various authors and were written at various
times for various purposes. No central theme or
organizing idea directed the authors, yet through
most a theme emerges. The uniting thread running
through all but the first paper is Vietnamese
nationalism.

The first paper, which alone concerns the
period of "traditional" Vietnam (during its age of
independence from the tenth to the early nineteenth
century), discusses Vietnamese society before the
impact of the Western concept of nationalism. Most
writers have typified this period of Vietnamese
history as one in which Chinese Confucianism was the
dominant idea and organizing principle in Vietnamese
society. Professor Smith takes a closer look at
this generalization and perceives that, as in China
itself, Confucianism in Vietnam varied in strength
and content through history. In Vietnam Smith

postulates a cyclical pattern of Confucian strength,
with periods of Confucian orthodoxy alternating
with periods of absence of commitment to any political philosophy. Smith suggests that this cyclical
interpretation may still have relevance in North
Vietnam today, accounting for the fluctuations in
policy between Marxist orthodoxy and nonphilosophic
pragmatism.

The next four papers presented here cluster in
time around the first two decades of the twentieth
century. This was an era during which affairs in
Vietnam, and, indeed, in Southeast Asia in general,
attracted scant notice outside the offices of colonial administrators. This was an era during which
Southeast Asia was regarded, if it was regarded at
all, as the epitome of peace, order, and profitable
production. This view of Southeast Asia was, of
course, the view of the colonial power, the colonial
governor, the colonial investor. This was the view
that "mattered."

World War II not only transformed the history
of the area--encouraging nationalist leaders and
movements that weakened the colonial power both
physically and psychologically, leading to removal
of Western rule from one-time colonies--but it
transformed the historical view of what was important before the war. The meteoric rise of national

heroes such as Hồ Chí Minh, Sukarno, and Aung San, leading mass movements and politicized populations, produced a scholarly search for antecedents in the deceptive calm of the prewar years. This second look at peaceful, orderly, and productive Southeast Asia revealed a Southeast Asia in which resistance to the West had never died, in which indigenous cultures had been continually fighting for survival and a new expression, in which Western means had been conceptualized as contributing to Asian ends.

The essays in this volume by Hoàng Ngọc Thành, Vũ Đức Bằng, William H. Frederick, and Milton Osborne are parts of the growing literature that is making understandable the transformation of seas of apparent tropic tranquillity into raging oceans of revolution.

The sixth and final paper, by Dr. Trường Bửu Lâm, also focuses on the theme of nationalism, but it brings the subject forward in time to the wartime years of the 1940s. The special relationship between the French and the Japanese had unique effects on nationalism in Vietnam and served to hinder rather than to foster the growth of a unified nationalist sentiment.

A word about the authors and their articles:

Dr. Ralph Smith, Lecturer in the History of Southeast Asia in the School of Oriental and African Studies, University of London, is the author of

Viet-Nam and the West (Cornell, 1971) and of several
articles on Vietnamese history. His essay here was
written for presentation at the University of Hawaii
during the week he spent as consultant to and guest
of Southeast Asian Studies, Asian Studies Program,
in 1970.

Dr. Vũ Đức Bằng produced his article on "The
Đông Kinh Free School Movement," 1907-1908 as a
master's thesis in education for his degree in Hawaii
in 1969. Mr. Bằng completed a Ph.D. degree in
education at the University of California at Los
Angeles in 1971. He has recently returned to Vietnam.

The article "Alexandre Varenne and Politics in
Indochina, 1925-26" was written by Mr. William H.
Frederick for a seminar in Southeast Asian history
at the University of Hawaii in 1968. Mr. Frederick
is now completing research for his dissertation
on the history of Surabaja between 1930 and 1950.

The fourth article, "The Faithful Few: The
Politics of Collaboration in Cochinchina in the
1920s" by Dr. Milton Osborne, was produced under the
same auspices as the first article by Dr. Smith;
that is, it was written for presentation at the University of Hawaii during the week he served as guest
consultant to Southeast Asian Studies of the Asian
Studies Program. Dr. Osborne is currently a member

of the History Department at American University.
He is author of *The French Presence in Cochinchina
and Cambodia* (Cornell, 1969) and of several articles
on Vietnamese and Cambodian history.

Dr. Hoàng Ngọc Thành, who received his doctoral
degree in history at the University of Hawaii in
1968, is currently a member of the faculty at the
University of Saigon. His essay "Quốc Ngữ and the
Development of Modern Vietnamese Literature" is
extracted from his dissertation, "The Social and
Political Development of Vietnam as Seen Through the
Modern Novel." Dr. Thành has also published several
books and articles in Vietnamese on the history of
his country.

Dr. Trường Bửu Lâm, who is Associate Professor
of History at the University of Hawaii, held the
post of Director of the Institute of Historical
Research, Ministry of National Education, in Saigon
for many years. He subsequently served as a research
associate at Harvard, Yale, and Cornell universities.
Professor Lâm's publications include *Patterns of
Vietnamese Response to Foreign Intervention* (Yale,
1967) and a number of articles on various other
aspects of Vietnamese history.

In addition to expressing its gratitude to the
author-contributors whose studies comprise this
volume, Southeast Asian Studies wishes to acknowledge

the efforts of many individuals who made this publication possible, in particular, those who organized the Vietnam consultations, seminars, and forums that were held in Hawaii in 1970: Professors Thomas Gething, Philip Jenner, Stephen O'Harrow, Fred W. Riggs, and Robert Van Niel.

Special thanks are owed to Professor Stephen O'Harrow, of the University's Indo-Pacific Languages Department, who supplied the diacritics of words transcribed in quốc ngữ.

Walter F. Vella

THE CYCLE OF CONFUCIANIZATION IN VIETNAM

By R. B. Smith

PART I

Vietnam has, more than once, been called a cross-roads of civilization. Quite apart from its encounter with the civilization of the West, which began in the seventeenth century, it lay between two very different cultural worlds--on the one hand, that of China, to whose emperor Vietnamese rulers paid regular tribute for centuries until 1883; and, on the other hand, that of Southeast Asia, with which it is increasingly associated by Western scholars. The relationship to Southeast Asia is more than artificial. Linguistically, Vietnamese is related to Khmer and Thai at least as closely as to Chinese, and some of Vietnam's institutions, notably the village *đình*, have close affinities with those of the hill peoples of the "Annamite Chain," whom ethnographers regard as Indonesian. Moreover, the southern part of the country was only drawn into the Sino-Vietnamese cultural sphere in the seventeenth century--that is, just as recently as the period in which Vietnam first came into contact with the West.

1

Nevertheless, in terms of literate civilization, the Vietnamese belong to the area in which Chinese was the dominant classical language, and even their vernacular language was first written in characters based on Chinese principles. This was because the northern part of the country was a province of China from the second century B.C. till the tenth century A.D. and for the next thousand years was occupied by a state which maintained political independence of China (apart from the payment of tribute), but which continued to draw its cultural inspiration from the Middle Kingdom.

It is with one aspect of this cultural inspiration that the present paper is concerned. But at the outset it must be remarked that *Chinese inspiration* and *Confucianism* are not necessarily synonymous terms which can always be substituted for one another. For one thing, Vietnam also acquired Buddhism from China, although at an early stage in the eastward spread of that religion, Vietnam probably played its own part in the development of Chinese Buddhism. It should also be remembered that in China, itself, Confucianism developed over the centuries and was not always so dominant as it was under the dynasties of Ming and Ch'ing. It would be a serious error for the historian of Vietnam, while being conscious of Chinese influence, to take China

2

too much for granted or to assume that China itself
was an unchanging model for Vietnam to imitate.
Chinese historiography has by now completely
escaped from the notion of the "cycle of Cathay,"
and Vietnamese historiography must take that into
account. When one comes to speak of "Confucianization" in Vietnam, one must remember that it was a
process which China also went through, and not
necessarily at a very much earlier period.

But what is meant if one says that Vietnam by
the mid-nineteenth century, at the latest, was a
Confucian state or, perhaps more correctly, a Neo-
Confucian state? The answer to this question must,
of course, lie partly in the definition of Confucianism (or Neo-Confucianism). There is not space in the
present paper to attempt such a definition, nor is
it necessary, since one can refer to several works
in English which deal with the subject at length.[1]
In brief, it can be stated that Confucianism was an
aspiration to have order obtain at all levels of society; to ensure that the individual, the family,
and the state were in harmony with Heaven and Earth
and the Five Agents of the universe. Without going
into detail, one can observe, therefore, that a
Confucian state was one in which the government
sought, by edicts and decrees, to ensure that everyone observed the requirements of propriety (*li*). We

have here, thus, one practical measure or indicator of the Confucian state: when Vietnamese rulers were insisting on propriety, Confucianism was probably strong; when Confucianism was weak, propriety would have mattered less. Another indicator, given the nature of Chinese historical writing, might be the occasions on which Vietnamese rulers ordered the compilation of historical records; for historical writing was very often another way in which attention was drawn to the virtues and failings of mankind, judged by Confucian standards.

These indicators alone, however, are not enough as a guide to the Confucianization of Vietnam. Whether a state followed Confucian principles or not depended not only on the content of Confucianism itself, but also on the character of its rulers. It would be quite wrong to see the Confucian state as one in which every single individual had been converted to Confucianism in the way that medieval Western states were converted to Christianity and might then be called Christian states. The Confucian state, rather, was one in which life was regulated and political decisions made by an elite of scholars, recruited through examinations based on the Confucian classics. And it is the presence or absence, and the relative power, of Confucian scholars that must be taken as the principal indicator of Confucianization.

4

It is because there were some periods when such scholars were powerful, and other periods when they were not, that it is possible to speak of a cycle of Confucianization in Vietnam. Nor should one think of monarchy as being specifically Confucian, although it was only through the monarch that scholars could control the country. There were elements of Taoism in the religious function of monarchy, which Confucians may have disapproved of, but which they were unable to remove. Monarchy was the keystone of traditional government both in China and in Southeast Asia; what the Confucian scholars had to do, if they were to ensure that the country was ruled according to their principles, was to capture the throne. The alternative was that it would be captured by some other kind of elite. Thus, Confucianization must be seen also in terms of political struggle between the scholars and other political groups, such as the army or the adepts of some religious sect. Having said all this in general terms, let us now consider the history of Confucianization in Vietnam between the eleventh and nineteenth centuries.

PART II

The key to the development of an elite of scholar-

officials was the examination system. In China, the
first origins of this institution may be found under
the Former Han dynasty, but its continuous history
began under the Sui dynasty, around 600 A.D. By the
later Sung period (say, the eleventh and twelfth
centuries), when Đại-Việt first became established
as an independent state, the examination system was
an essential part of the Chinese governmental framework, with the *chin-shih* degree being the highest
qualification for official status. But it was not
until the early Ming period that the examinations
finally superseded all other roads to bureaucratic
appointment and the expansion of education made the
Confucian classics the basis of an all-embracing
orthodoxy.[2]

In Vietnam, the first reference to an examination occurs in the *Đại-Việt Sử-Ký Toàn-Thư* under the
year 1075; a second reference occurs under 1086.
But, while these references do seem to indicate the
practice of choosing scholars by examination in the
capital and the existence of a Hàn-Lâm-Viện (Han Lin
Academy) by the latter date, they cannot be taken as
evidence of a regular trienniel examination system.
The third reference comes about a century later, in
1185, when we learn from the same source that thirty
men were chosen by examination to be allowed to study
in the capital.[3] After that, we have to wait until

6

1232, when the chronicle mentions the names of five laureates, in an examination which is not in any way stated to be an innovation of that year.[4] This was the first of seven examinations in the first half of the Trần period, given between the years 1232 and 1304, in which an increasing number of laureates (including the five mentioned above) appear.[5] Thus, one can say that, by the Trần period (corresponding to the later years of the Southern Sung in China), an examination system was established in Vietnam. It is clear, too, that some of the laureates later rose to high positions in the state, although we have no means of knowing what their social origins were, and therefore how much they owed to education and how much to birth. But there can be no doubt that during the thirteenth and fourteenth centuries the dominant position in Vietnamese society and government belonged to the imperial clan and its relatives, and not to any group of people chosen by examination.

Under the Trần dynasty, until at least 1320, the imperial clan succeeded in guaranteeing peaceful successions by a system of abdication of emperors, which meant that power usually lay with the emperor's father, as thượng-hoàng ('the emperor above'); and there is no example from that period of an emperor's allowing a female member of any other clan to gain

power for her relatives by becoming queen. In the
thirteenth century, the dominant positions belonged
quite clearly to the Trần princes bearing noble
titles such as *đại-vương* and *vương*, with descent in
rank at each generation. In this period, laureates
from examinations would have little chance to become
powerful figures, and, so far as one can see, none
did. Đại-Việt was much more monarchical (and also
Buddhist) than Confucian. Even in the fourteenth
century, the way in which the Trần monopoly of power
broke down was through the rise of another clan (the
Lê of Thanh-Hóa, forerunners of Lê Quý Ly), which at
last succeeded in placing a female member on the
queen's throne and so was able eventually to claim
blood relationship to the emperor. In 1369 Đại-Việt
experienced its first succession crisis, in which
two princes vied for the throne with the support of
conflicting court factions. The previous emperor's
nominee was overthrown by an army from the province
of Thanh-Hóa which was led by Trần princes, but
which relied on the support of the Lê clan. There-
upon, the mother of the defeated candidate fled to
Champa and was able to secure a Cham attack on Hanoi
in 1374.[6] During the war with Champa that followed,
the leader who emerged in Đại-Việt was Lê Quý Ly, who
was powerful enough by the end of the century to
seize the throne for his own family, inaugurating

the short-lived Hồ dynasty. In the Trần period Đại-
Việt was thus in no sense a Confucian state: Bud-
dhism still flourished, and, although it was Chinese
(Mahayana) Buddhism, the Vietnamese monarchy was not
at this period fundamentally different from, say,
the Buddhist monarchy of the Mon-Thai state, of which
Ayutthaya became the capital in 1350. Indeed, the
latter experienced a succession crisis of its own in
1369 which was remarkably similar to that of Đại-
Việt's in the same year. It was with the growth of
Theravada Buddhism in Siam and Confucianization in
Vietnam (only just beginning in the fourteenth
century) that the sharp cultural contrast between
the two areas in modern times began to take shape.

To return to the examinations, in 1374 (five
years after the triumph of the Ming in China) we find
reference to a Vietnamese examination in which it is
stated that the custom was for thirty laureates to
be chosen every seven years, though only three are
named.[7] We have no means of knowing whether this
represents an actual innovation, but certainly there
were further examinations in 1384, 1393, 1400, and
1405--not precisely at seven-year intervals, but,
nevertheless, the largest number of examinations so
far within a thirty-year period.[8] It is probably
from this time that we can date the continuous
history of the Vietnamese examination system. But,

9

as we shall see, that history was by no means smooth
throughout the centuries which followed.

It was in the fifteenth century that Confucian
scholarship began to dominate the Vietnamese polity.
Probably the Ming occupation of the greater part of
the country between 1407 and 1427 played some part in
this. For those twenty years, Vietnam was again a
Chinese province, and during that time it sent 161
"tribute students" to the Chinese capital to study
for the examinations.[9] To judge from the location
of the schools founded by the Ming administration,
probably most of the students were from Tongking.
In that area, but not farther south, the Ming period
saw a deepening of Confucian culture.

But it was not the Confucian-educated scholars
who drove the Chinese out of Đại-Việt; it was the
growing body of followers of Lê Lợi, whose leaders
eventually emerged as a military elite with its roots
in the province of Thanh-Hóa. The success of Lê Lợi
meant an interruption of the rise of the scholar-
officials: the politics of Đại-Việt in the period
between 1428 and 1460 revolved around a conflict
between "counselors" (*đại-thần*), who were mainly
military men from Thanh-Hóa, and "scholar-officials"
(*quan*). This conflict has been studied in great
detail by Dr. J. K. Whitmore and therefore need not
be described in detail here.[10] What is important

in the present context is that later, during the
first decade of his reign, Lê Thánh-Tông (1460-97)
was able to achieve a new political stability in his
kingdom, within which, for the first time, political
and administrative power came into the hands of the
scholar-officials. It is probably a mistake to see
this as the work of the emperor, alone; rather, it
was the result of a situation in which an emperor
who had been educated by Confucian scholars was
placed on the throne by an alliance between a
military court faction and the leading scholars.
Such, at least, would appear to have been the nature
of the *xướng-nghĩa* coup of 1460. By 1470 the scholars were firmly in the saddle. They reformed the
structure of government in such a way as to give
primacy to the "six boards" and to the Hàn-Lâm
Academy, from which they were staffed. They insisted
on a more serious observation of customary rites,
including proper mourning periods and sacrifices to
the cult of Confucius; and they limited the number
of Buddhist temples. Above all, in 1463 they introduced regular triennial examinations, in which *tiến-
sĩ* (*chin-shih*) laureates were selected to fill the
growing number of administrative positions made
necessary by other reforms. Between 1463 and 1514
there was no break in the triennial pattern, and in
those eighteen examinations as many as eight hundred

sixteen laureates were selected.

The spirit of that court is reflected also in
the literary history of the country. The emperor
established a literary group at court, the Tao-Đàn,
whose poetry still survives in both Vietnamese and
Chinese, and the Hồng-Đức reign (1470-97) is regarded
as the Golden Age of Confucian scholarship in Vietnam. Among its products may be mentioned the encyclopedic collection finished in 1483, the *Thiên-Nam
Dư Hạ Tập*, and the *Đại-Việt Sử-Ký Toàn-Thư*, a history
of Vietnam by Ngô Sĩ Liên, which was commissioned in
1479. The latter, significantly, includes commentaries by Ngô Sĩ Liên on chronicles of earlier
periods which reveal a strong Confucian concern that
things were not done properly under the Ly and Trần
dynasties.

All this, however, cannot be presented as the
final establishment of Confucianism as the unifying
orthodoxy of Vietnam. Had that been the case, the
title of the present paper would be meaningless. In
fact, the Confucianization of the fifteenth century
was all but undone by the end of the sixteenth.
Two factors combined to produce this result--the
tendency toward clan conflict which was inherent in
the Vietnamese tradition and the gradual expansion
of Vietnamese settlement, which meant that there was
always a frontier area where Confucian scholarship

12

was not firmly established. Dr. Whitmore's analysis of the conflicts of the period between 1428 and 1460 has shown that it was the military men of Thanh-Hóa who were most unwilling to see power fall into the hands of the scholar-officials of the Tongking Delta. Thanh-Hóa was a province which had relatively recently come under extensive Vietnamese settlement; when the scholars finally had their way, in the 1460s, it is significant that in the first examination (in 1463) only five of forty-four laureates came from Thanh-Hóa, the rest being from the four provinces of the Tongking.[11] Presumably, during the course of the reign of Lê Thánh-Tông, Confucianism became stronger in the South, but it is unlikely that the contrast between the two areas was completely eliminated.

The tendency toward clan conflict came to the fore in the early sixteenth century. By the year 1509, there were two parties contending for power at Hanoi, one with its roots in Tongking, and the other associated with Thanh-Hóa; each had female members who were imperial wives or widows. In 1509 the throne was seized by a Lê prince whose support lay in Thanh-Hóa, and the Tongking party was driven from power. But, then, in 1516 there was a major rebellion in Tongking, when the throne was briefly seized by Trần Cao (who claimed descent from the

Trần emperors). He was driven out in a matter of
days, but in the conflicts which followed, a number
of clans emerged as centers of power, including the
Trịnh and the Nguyễn, with their roots in Thanh-Hóa,
and the Mạc, whose power-base was in Tongking.[12]
Yet, despite the fact that none of these clans was
involved in scholarship, the examination system did
not completely break down. The examination due to
have been held in 1517 was postponed till the following year; but a further one was held in 1518, and
thereafter the triennial pattern was resumed. Nor
did the system break down in 1527, when the Mạc
finally seized the throne and deposed the Lê ruler.
The triennial examinations continued in Tongking
throughout the Mạc period (1527-92), with the sole
exception of the year 1559, when there was an attack
on the capital from the South. The number of laureates was smaller, and quite probably they held less
power than in the Hồng-Đức period; but they were by
no means eliminated.

However, the Mạc did not succeed in controlling
the whole of Đại-Việt. In 1534 the Lê emperor was
restored in Thanh-Hóa by the two powerful clans of
that area, the Nguyễn and the Trịnh, and from then
till 1592 there were two rival monarchs in Đại-Việt.
The one in the South was much less Confucian. The
Lê court did, in fact, hold eight examinations

14

between 1554 and 1592, but they received, at the most, only sixty-five laureates throughout that period, compared with the two hundred twenty who succeeded in the twelve examinations held by the Mạc during that time. It is not surprising that when the Mạc were finally driven from Hanoi by the armies of the Lê-Trịnh-Nguyễn party in 1592, the examination system ceased to be an important element in the system of Vietnamese government for a time. But it did not, even then, go out of existence altogether. Triennial examinations were held at Hanoi through most of the seventeenth century, but in the forty years from 1595 to 1634 there were only ninety-three laureates--fewer than seven per examination, compared with an average of forty-five per examination between 1463 and 1514. The pattern is indicated more clearly in table 1.

TABLE 1

EXAMINATION LAUREATES (*Tiến-Sĩ*), 1463-1691

	Number of Examinations	Number of Laureates	Average Number of Laureates Per Examination
1463-1514	18	816	45
1518-53	13	330	25
1556-92 (Mac only)	12	220	18-19
1595-1634	13	93	7
1637-91	19	270	14

SOURCE: *Đại-Việt Lịch-Triều Đăng-Khoa-Lục* (Saĩgon, 1963).

The declining importance of the examinations in the first half of the seventeenth century coincides with other indicators of the relative unimportance of Confucianism. For one thing, it was a remarkably thin period in literary history. Hardly any important authors were writing at that time, either in Vietnamese (*chữ nôm*) or in Chinese. Secondly, it was a period of renewed Buddhist activity, which may or may not be coincidental. Clearly, Buddhism had not completely died out in Vietnam as a result of the decree of 1461 which had sought to limit its expansion. But it seems to have received very little encouragement from the court during the succeeding

16

century and a half. When the writer Trần Văn Giáp searched the *Cương-Mục* chronicle for references to Buddhism, he found only one between 1465 and the early seventeenth century, and that related to the repair of a pagoda in 1498.[13] But in the early decades of the seventeenth century we once again find references to new sects and to the arrival of Buddhist monks from China. Trịnh Tráng, virtual ruler of northern Vietnam between 1623 and 1657, seems to have been a patron of Buddhism, and the empress of Lê Thần-Tông (1619-43) was converted to that religion by a Chinese monk in the 1630s. The same trend is noticeable in the southern part of the country (what is now Central Vietnam), where the Nguyễn clan established virtually an independent state after 1600. The Nguyễn ruler Hiền-Vương, who reigned from 1648 to 1687, was a notable Buddhist, and gave protection to a number of monks who fled from China after the fall of the Ming.[14] In both areas, the importance of Buddhism continued into the eighteenth century.

The figures in table 1 suggest a slight recovery of Confucianism during the latter part of the seventeenth century, at least in the northern half of the country. The reason for this is by no means clear, for, as yet, the politics of the seventeenth century have not been studied in the detail with

17

which Dr. Whitmore has explored those of the fifteenth. There was a marked revival from 1659, and
in the examinations between then and 1691 there
were only three occasions when the total did not
reach ten or more--in 1670, it reached 31. This
revival, moreover, coincided with other events during
the rule of Trịnh Tạc (1657-82). In 1662 he published "Instructions for the Reform of Customs," a
severely Confucian proclamation which was critical
of both Buddhism and Christianity and which was
followed by an active persecution of Christians.[15]
The following year, Phạm Công Trứ and other scholars
were commissioned to revise and extend the *Đại-Việt
Sử-Ký Toàn-Thư* (which was finished by 1665, though
not published till 1697). And in 1664 the same
official came forward with proposals for the reform
of taxation. One has the impression of a new spirit
in government and scholarship, though not of the
same vigor as that seen under Lê Thánh-Tông.

    With the eighteenth century, we come to a period
for which no examination figures are readily available, but in which there is other evidence of period-
ic conflict between Confucian scholars and their
non-Confucian enemies. During the 1720s there are
indications of a new, more rigorous approach to the
country's growing financial problems, in which the
lead would seem to have been taken by a *Tongkingese*

official. It is even possible that the officials were able to gain in power at the expense of the Trịnh clan. But in 1731 and 1732 a new Trịnh ruler, Trịnh Giang (1729-40), reasserted his family's power by having the Lê emperor put to death, and the attempted reforms were abandoned.[16] What is remarkable is that after his coup there was a period in which Buddhism flourished and Confucianism did not: In 1734, Trịnh Giang forbade the importation of Confucian texts from China, but shortly afterwards sent a mission to obtain Buddhist texts. Three years later he forced the court to make donations for a large image of Buddha for an important pagoda. Although the examinations probably went on, it was at this period that offices were first sold for cash in Vietnam. It is hardly surprising that in 1738 there was a revolt in Tongking aimed at a Lê restoration, which led to a prolonged period of rebellion in certain areas. It is to be hoped that in due course these events will become the subject of detailed study, for the period presents a fascinating opportunity to look at traditional Vietnamese politics in action. Far less information is available concerning the internal development of what is now Central Vietnam during the seventeenth and eighteenth centuries, when it was under the rule of the Nguyễn clan and virtually independent of Hanoi. We

19

know that reorganizations of the country occurred
in 1702 and 1744, but their precise character is
obscure. However, it seems very unlikely that
Confucianism was dominant in the Nguyễn provinces
at that time.

One fact about the eighteenth century is very
clear, however: whatever degree of Confucianization
had been achieved by about 1770, either in the
North or in the South, was totally disrupted by the
events which followed the Tây-Sơn rebellion of 1774.
By 1790, none of the three centers of government in
Vietnam was strongly Confucian: Hanoi, under the
Tây-Sơn emperor Quang-Trung (who also built a new
capital in Nghệ-An province); Qui-Nhơn, under his
brother, who was ruling as Thái-Đức; or Saigon,
where the last survivor of the Nguyễn clan had just
reestablished himself. Quang-Trung is noted for his
decision to make *chữ nôm* (Vietnamese) the language
of administration instead of Chinese--which does
not suggest any strong attachment to the Confucian
classics--while Nguyễn Ánh depended a great deal
on the support of a group of French mercenaries
raised for him by the Catholic missionary Pigneau de
Behaine. It was Nguyễn Ánh who unified Vietnam in
1802 and ruled over it until 1820 with the reign-
title Gia-Long. Even with the return of peace,
therefore, and in spite of a revival of local and

provincial examinations in 1807, there was no sudden
return to Confucian orthodoxy.

This came with the death of Gia-Long and the
accession of his son Minh-Mạng, who, like Lê Thánh-
Tông, had been educated by Confucian scholars. Dr.
A. B. Woodside has drawn attention to the completely
different characters of Minh-Mạng's reign and that
of his predecessor.[17] Indeed, the years from 1820 to
1847 (under Minh-Mạng and Thiệu-Trị) saw a pattern
of Confucianization not at all unlike that of the
period from 1460 to 1497. The examination system
was revived (see table 2), and the number of laureates increased from decade to decade. The machinery
of government was overhauled, with a key role being
played by the Nội-Các (Grand Secretariat), closely
linked to the Hàn-Lâm Academy.[18] A new historical
office was established, which produced the Veritable
Records (*thực-lục*) of the dynasty and later the
Khâm-Định Việt-Sử Thông-Giám Cương-Mục, which summarized Vietnamese history down to 1789. Moreover,
as time went on, it is clear from the records of
examination successes that by the middle of the
century Confucian education was establishing itself
in the provinces of Central Vietnam, and even
beginning to count for something in the Far South.

TABLE 2

EXAMINATION LAUREATES, 1822-80

A. BY PERIOD

	Number of Examinations	Number of Laureates
Minh-Mạng (1822-41)	6	66
Thiệu-Trị (1841-47)	5	79
Tự-Đức		
(1848-56)	5	93
(1862-80)	9	112
TOTAL 58 years	25	360

B. BY REGION OF BIRTH

Area	Total Number of Laureates, 1822-80
Tongking	150
Thanh-Hóa	16
Nghệ-Tĩnh	75
Central Annam	115
Lục-Tỉnh (Far South)	4
TOTAL	360

SOURCE: *Quốc-Triều Đăng-Khoa-Lục* (Saïgon, 1962), *passim*.

Two other indications of the growth of Confucian orthodoxy under Minh-Mạng and his successors may be cited. The first is reflected in a series of measures taken with regard to the land system of Bình Định province in 1839.[19] Their purpose was to try to increase the amount of communal land possessed by each village and reduce the extent of privately owned land. The insistence that each village should have its communal land, which until 1724 was the only kind of land subject to land tax, was a peculiarly Vietnamese feature of the social system. Its origins are still somewhat obscure, but it does not appear to have derived from any Chinese example. Nevertheless, it fitted in well with the Confucian view of an ordered society, and it is therefore not surprising to find it being reinforced by imperial edict (albeit in relation to only one province) in the latter part of the reign of Minh-Mạng. The fundamental issues in Vietnamese Confucianization were whether and how society should be ordered and regulated from above. Insistence on communal property, which was regularly redivided among the inhabitants of a village, was an important element in that regulation.

The second manifestation of orthodoxy in this period was the growth of persecution of Christianity from 1825. Under Gia-Long Christianity had been

tolerated throughout Vietnam, and in the South it
was tolerated by Lê Văn Duyệt until his death in
1832. But in 1825 we find an edict against Christian missionaries and churches, which marks the
beginning of a trend that was to culminate in 1833
in a decree completely proscribing the Christian
religion.[20] This policy was maintained officially
(though the rigor of its application may have fluc-
tuated) from then until 1862, and it was one of the
principal reasons for French intervention in Vietnam.

PART III

It might be asked whether this theme of Confucianization in Vietnamese history has any relevance for
the study of more recent times. I think that it
may. Clearly, Confucianism itself, as a principle
of government, ceased to appeal to the Vietnamese
about the same time as it declined in China, although one might well apply to Vietnam some of the
thoughts on Chinese intellectual continuity developed
by the late Professor J. R. Levenson.[21] But what
has been said in the present paper about the fluc-
tuating fortunes of the Confucian scholars as a
political group may well reflect something deeper
than just the intellectual content of Confucian

24

philosophy. Confucianism is but one example of the
human tendencies to desire order in society and to
seek to discipline the individual according to principles whose first appeal is to the intellect,
rather than the heart. Is not communism equally
an example of the same tendency? If it is admitted
to be such, then perhaps communism has a similar
appeal to the Vietnamese mind and to a similar sort
of Vietnamese person.

Since 1954 in North Vietnam there has, in fact,
been a developing conflict between two tendencies
which have sometimes been identified with specific
personalities in the leadership. The conflict is
best reflected in the contrast (and, it would seem,
the mutual hostility) between Trường Chinh (Đặng
Xuân Khu) and Lê Duân. The former was secretary of
the Lao-Động party from 1951 until 1956 and, as
such, responsible for the policy of land reform
carried out during those years; Lê Duân has filled
virtually the same post since 1960, Hồ Chí Minh
having held it in the interval. The details of Hanoi
politics are beyond the reach of the Western scholar,
but observers seem agreed that, in general terms,
Trường Chinh stands for a more doctrinaire approach
to policy, and Lê Duân for a greater degree of pragmatism. These are surely the same opposing tendencies to be found in Vietnamese politics in the

fifteenth and, again, in the early nineteenth centuries.

Indeed, one might suggest that in many respects
the whole situation in North Vietnam between 1954
and, say, 1965 was comparable to that which had
existed in the first decade after the defeat of the
Chinese in 1427. Lê Lợi had driven out the Ming; Hồ
Chí Minh had led a successful campaign to drive out
the French. And, just as Lê Lợi was surrounded by a
following of men who had proved themselves militarily
rather than through scholarship, so Hồ Chí Minh was
supported by a group of men whose military daring
and organizational skill were probably more important
than their commitment to communism or any other
political philosophy. Nevertheless, there were in
the same movement men like Trường Chinh (dare one
compare him to Nguyễn Trãi, the only Tongkingese
scholar in Lê Lợi's close entourage?), for whom
Marxism as a philosophy mattered just as much as
Confucianism did to the fifteenth-century scholars.
The principal difference would be that in the fifteenth century the Confucians had the disadvantage
of being more closely associated with the Ming than
with Lê Lợi and were therefore deliberately kept out
of positions of influence for a generation, whereas
under Hồ Chí Minh military figures like Võ Nguyên
Giáp were united with the more doctrinaire Communists

26

in a single movement. Even so, after 1954 one finds
the same kind of rivalry between doctrine and pragmatism as after 1427. Might one anticipate the same
kind of result? In the fifteenth century, when the
generation of military leaders who had actually
fought the Chinese died away, their successors could
not prevent the reemergence--stronger than ever--of
Confucian scholars. Is it possible that as time
goes on (assuming an eventual return to peace) a new
generation of doctrinaire Communists will take over?

[1]For example, see W. de Bary, Ed., *Sources of Chinese Tradition* (New York: Columbia University Press, 1960), and Wing-tsit Chan, *A Source Book in Chinese Philosophy* (Princeton: Princeton University Press, 1963).

[2]Compare W. Franke, *The Reform and Abolition of the Traditional Chinese Examination System* (Cambridge, Mass.: Harvard University Press, 1960), and Ho Ping-ti, *The Ladder of Success in Imperial China* (New York: Columbia University Press, 1962).

[3]*Đại-Việt Sử-Ký Toàn-Thư* (Vietnamese translation, Hanoi, 1967), 1:236, 240, 295.

[4]Ibid., 2:12.

[5]*Đại-Việt Lịch-Triều Đăng-Khoa-Lục* (Vietnamese translation, Saigon, 1963), pp. 13-17.

[6]*Toàn-Thư*, 2:153 ff.

[7]Ibid., p. 165.

[8]*Lịch-Triều Đang-Khoa-Lục*. pp. 18 ff.

[9]A. B. Woodside, "Early Ming Expansionism: China's Abortive Conquest of Vietnam," *Papers on China*, (Cambridge, Mass.: Harvard University, 1963), 17:1-37.

[10]J. K. Whitmore, "The Development of Le Government in Fifteenth Century Viet-Nam" (Ph.D. diss., Cornell University, 1968).

[11]Ibid., p. 129.

[12]The complexities of the period between 1505 and 1527 are analyzed in Phan Huy Le, *Lịch-Sử Chế-Độ Phong-Kiến Việt-Nam* (Hanoi, 1962), 2:222-44.

[13]Trần Văn Giáp, "Le Bouddhisme en Annam," *BEFEO*, vol. 32 (1932):191-268.

[14]E. Gaspardone, "Bonzes des Ming refugies en Annam," *Sinologica* vol. 2 (1950):12-30.

[15]Translation by R. Deloustal, *BEFEO* 10 (1910): 23-33.

[16]For details of the decrees of this period, see R. Deloustal, "Ressources Financières et Econom-iques de l'Etat dans l'Ancien Annam," *Revue Indo-chinoise*, n.s. vol. 42-43 (1924).

[17]A. B. Woodside, "Some Features of the Viet-namese Bureaucracy Under the Early Nguyễn Dynasty," *Papers on China*, vol. 19 (Cambridge, Mass.: Harvard University, 1965).

[18]See the detailed study of the memorial system in Chen Ching-ho, "The Imperial Archives of the Nguyễn Dynasty," *JSEAH* 3, no. 2 (September 1962): 111-28.

[19]Nguyễn Thiệu Lâu, "La Reforme Agraire de 1839 dans le Bình-Định," *BEFEO* vol. 45 (1951).

[20]G. Taboulet, *La Geste Française en Indochine* (Paris, 1955), 1:322, 327-29.

[21]J. R. Levenson, *Confucian China and Its Modern Fate*, 3 vols. (London, 1958-65).

THE ĐÔNG KINH FREE SCHOOL MOVEMENT, 1907-1908

By Vũ Đức Bằng

> Really, it is time that France put on
> this land her stamp which is civilization
> itself.[1]   --P. Doumer
>
> Your country (France) belongs to the
> seas of the West, ours to those of the
> East. . . As the horse and the buffalo
> differ, so do we--in language, literature,
> customs. . . If you persist in putting the
> torch to us, disorder will be long.[2]
>   --Anonymous

It is generally agreed that the first systematic
modernization of colonial Vietnam began with Governor
General Paul Doumer (1897-1902). From the time the
French troops had first occupied Saigon in 1859 until
the arrival of Doumer in 1897, the French "presence"
in Vietnam had meant thirty-eight long and bloody
years of "pacification."

Doumer, strongly believing in an all-out mobili-
zation of modern means to crush the last strongholds
of Vietnamese resistance, set out to provide the
country with a network of communications, with
fiscal reforms, and with political centralization.
This modern administrative apparatus helped France
toward two major gains. First, the nationalists,[3]
now faced with a foe immeasurably superior in modern
technology, were fighting a losing battle. Doumer,

in his political report of 1901, could safely boast that "since 1897, none of our Indochinese troops have died."[4] The second important gain for France was that with the great economic equipment which Doumer provided them the Indochinese states ceased to be a financial burden to France. In that same political report of 1901, Doumer proudly announced that the general budget of Indochina, then well in excess, could secure a net deposit of "nearly thirty million (francs) in the reserve funds."[5]

Yet, even if Doumer's gigantic scheme to modernize Indochina appeared impressive in the eyes of the natives and did add some prestige to France, it was regarded by the Vietnamese nationalists as utterly artificial and irrelevant. The population was not prepared for it. Doumer's sophisticated bridges and highways did not improve the lot of the Vietnamese peasants any more than the creation by his predecessors of the Tongking Academy or the Hanoi Opera had.[6] For education, Doumer did almost nothing. Again, in his famous report he merely pointed out the French mistake in the past of having greatly upset the institutions of "a country of ancient civilization" and candidly observed that "in spite of recent studies and the concern we do have, we must confess that the formula for a French education for the natives has not been found thus far."[7]

Instead, Doumer brought upon the Vietnamese people unbearable forced labor, heavy taxes, excessive centralization, notorious cruelty by the colonials-- all that harassed the masses and exacerbated mandarins and scholars. Increasing nationalist agitation was the result.

With a new Governor General, Jean Baptiste Paul Beau (1902-1908), replacing Paul Doumer, nationalist agitation grew more overt after Vietnam had suffered three successive disastrous harvests and subsequent devaluation of the piaster. To combat the universal dissatisfaction, Beau then launched his so-called moral conquest, concentrating his reforms in the two fronts of education and medical service. In a speech delivered on March 28, 1905, Beau declared, "The hour has come to substitute the policy of association for the policy of domination."[8]

Yet, the hour had come too late. Confronted with the strong opposition of well-entrenched colonials, Governor General Beau's works of reform were slow and insufficient. Furthermore, the Japanese victory over the Russians in 1905 awakened dormant national feelings and healed the natives' injured pride at being subdued for years by the West. Vietnam's scholars,[9] now in a furious mood, were awakened to the hard fact that only rapid modernization could

32

help the country evict the French.

All this was skillfully exploited by a nationalist militant, a master in psychological maneuvering, Phan Bội Châu (1867-1940). In 1900 with a few
other patriots Phan Bội Châu had already founded his
New party, which was the embryo of Vietnam's first
modern political party, the Association for the
Modernization of Vietnam, which Châu also founded,
in 1905. In 1904, with his *New Book Written with
Tears of Blood from Ryukyu,* in which he compared
the unhappy lot of his country to the fate that had
befallen the Ryukyu Islands under Japanese domination, Phan Bội Châu rallied an increasing number of
leading scholars to his cause, among them Phan Châu
Trinh (1872-1926) and Lương Văn Can (1854-1927).

Phan Bội Chau did not stay to hear Governor
General Beau's speech or witness how he carried
out his "association package."[10] Instead, he went
to Japan early in 1905 to witness the splendid
harvest of Japan's Westernization on the spot.
Struck by Japan's remarkable progress, Phan Bội
Châu eventually appealed to his fellow countrymen to
come observe "the miracle of the Rising Sun" more
closely, with him. Thus, a number of scholars and
students managed to flee the country to study in
Japan with Châu. Both on-the-spot witnesses and
hearers at home vowed to imitate Japan in modernizing

33

Vietnam. In keeping with a tradition which had always put learning at the core of national development and in contrast to French modernization, which had neglected education, this group which now called itself the Tokyo group made education the very foundation of Vietnam's modernization. Furthermore, to provide this foundation with necessary breadth and support, they appealed to the masses in a nationwide campaign for mass education. They began with the opening of a modest private school, the Đông Kinh Nghĩa Thục, which grew steadily into a full-fledged movement known as the Đông Kinh Free School Movement.

The movement, limited in its resources and foiled in its final stages of development by the French, had only a short life. However, it showed enough originality, vigor, and maturity to truly deserve its place as "the first drive toward modernization and mass education of Vietnam."[11]

> If our people are treated badly and op-
> pressed as we are now, it is because,
> neglecting education, we are not as
> instructed and as intelligent as other
> peoples. . . The Japanese have aban-
> doned their old-fashioned customs and
> adopted the path of progress: They have
> created schools to teach their common
> people.[12]
>
> --Phan Bội Châu

One day in March 1907 a group of Hanoi boys and girls
entered a small flat at 4, Hàng Đào Street. This
modest setting was to be the birthplace of the first
Vietnamese private, nonsectarian, free school and
the center of a popular movement for educational
modernization and social reform known as the Đông
Kinh Free School movement. As its name suggests, the
school was free of tuition and provided the students
with textbooks and other school materials. Those
students born of poor families who demonstrated
academic ability were even provided a small scholarship. Both day and night classes were conducted, for
the convenience of students and teachers. There
were sleeping places for students whose homes were
some distance from the school. Free lunches were
served for less privileged students and for teachers.
Since the majority of teachers volunteered to teach
free, lunches were the only compensation the school
gave them. At its peak, enrollment at the Đông Kinh

Free School numbered around one thousand students, grouped into forty classes.[13]

The success of the new school was tremendous. For the first time--to the horror of conservative scholars--girls and boys shared their learning under the same roof. For the first time, also, modern education was advocated and disseminated by native teachers, who, unlike French masters, enjoyed the unreserved confidence and support of students and parents, alike. Classes at the Đông Kinh were filled to capacity. To provide new places, the school had to rent an adjoining flat. Students were drawn from all thirty-six of the sectors which then composed Hanoi. There were even students from suburban areas and beyond, who either stayed at the school for lunch and went home after their afternoon classes or stayed at the school overnight. In a very short time the school enjoyed a greater reputation than either the schools operated by the French or those sponsored by the imperial court at Huê.[14]

Parents, students, benefactors, and sympathizers of the Đông Kinh Free School were amazed at its success, but probably very few knew its origin. The genesis of the school can be traced to the kindling of the imagination of a nationalist during his short stay in an Asian country. Phan Châu Trinh, on a trip to Japan in early 1906, "discovered" and was

greatly amazed by one phenomenon in modern Japan, the
Keio Gijuku, a school founded by a great modernizer,
Yukichi Fukuzawa, which Trinh considered to be the
cradle of the Japanese drive for modernization.[15]
Back in Vietnam, Trinh and Phan Bội Châu, Tăng Bạt
Hổ[16] and Lương Văn Can unanimously agreed to open
such a school. The school was significantly named
Đông Kinh, or Tokyo.[17] Subsequent meetings resulted
in the election of Lương Văn Can and Nguyễn Quyền,
as director and principal of the new school, res-
pectively. Lương Văn Can, then more than fifty years
of age, was highly respected among scholars and
popularly called Cử Can because he had won a Cử-Nhân
(licentiate degree) in a regional literary competition. The principal, Nguyễn Quyền, a number of years
younger than the director, was popularly known as
Huấn Quyền because of his previous service as government Huấn Đạo (district school superintendent).[18]

The Đông Kinh staff was divided into four
departments: faculty, budget and finance, public
relations and advertising, and publications and
translations. The faculty, subdivided into various
sections, comprised teachers from the most hetero-
geneous backgrounds. The Chinese section had a large
array of talent in Chinese culture,[19] but the mathematics section was headed by a self-taught scholar,[20]
the drawing section by an employee at the City Geo-

graphical Services,[21] and the French-language section
by civil servants who were only available for teaching at night.[22] The Vietnamese section was handled
by two Vietnamese women teachers.[23]

The curriculum at Đông Kinh represented the
first private effort to give each teacher a special-
ty. Traditional teachers had used to be jacks-of-
all-trades, dispensing all skills and disciplines.
At Đông Kinh School, modern subjects for the first
time were enthusiastically advocated by the scholars,
who adopted them unanimously. Physical education,
mathematics, the rudiments of science and hygiene,
geography, political history and economy, civics,
and, especially, the native language constituted the
core of the curriculum.[24]

Students at Đông Kinh Free School were classi-
fied according not to their ages, but to their ability, into three levels using the modern terminology
"Tiểu, Trung, Đại" (primary, secondary, and higher
education). Primary students were those learning
their three R's, using the vernacular. Secondary
students were those who had mastered the vernacular
and now were beginning the rudiments of French. Students of higher education were those who were already
proficient in Chinese and were qualified to use
modern textbooks written by progressive Chinese
scholars like K'ang Yu-wei and Liang Ch'i-ch'ao.[25]

All modern forms and methods of instruction known and available to them at that time were put into use. Study of modern books, rhetorical declamations, lectures, discussions, and even newspapers was included in the schedule. In addition to academic courses, the school often organized topical lectures on specific issues, either political or educational. Lecturers were authorities within the circle of "progressive" scholars. French educators also came in and talked informally with the faculty and the more advanced students. Once in a while a student was assigned to present a talk on a historical or civic subject.[26] At the front entrance, fixed against the gate, was a suggestion box for students and guests to present their constructive ideas for further improvement of the school.[27]

In order to support the school financially, contributions from parents and benefactors were sought. However, the Đông Kinh attempted to stand on its feet through the creation of agricultural and commercial cooperatives among its members. These associations were organized rather loosely and were founded primarily to raise funds to send native students to Japan and China to study. Later they also aimed at assisting other free private schools, and they spread out considerably in number. However, due to the inexperience of the scholars, these

cooperatives did not make the financial situation
of the Đồng Kinh less precarious. It was reported
that at one time the wife of the school's director,
Mrs. Lương Văn Can, had to sell a shop of hers to
help defray the costs of the ever-growing school.[28]
Later, the contributions of members and benefactors,
poor and rich, grew more significant. When the
school was forced by the French to close its doors
for political reasons in December 1907, its budget
showed a substantial excess of over ten thousand
piasters, an amount then capable of running the
school for months.

> The French give to our institute of national
> learning a French name, try hard to teach
> us French, while neglecting the instruction
> of hundreds of useful skills like military
> science, mechanics, electrical engineering,
> and chemistry. Agricultural knowledge is
> primitive, commerce and industry completely
> naive.[29]
>
> --Phan Bội Châu

The circumstances then in Vietnam appeared to be
quite favorable for the opening of a free and private
modern school. After Paul Beau had succeeded Paul
Doumer as Indochina's governor general in 1902,
French policy clearly had encouraged the establishment of private educational institutions "to compete," as Beau put it, "with the missionaries'
schools" and "to seize control of one of the most
important factors of the colonial policy."[30]

Beau's apparent efforts to improve native education impressed a great number of nationalists.
Thus far, the French contribution to Vietnamese
education had been limited to a number of schools
for training interpreters and a few Franco-indige-
nous schools which concentrated on training office
clerks.[31] As it turned out, the traditional system
was greatly disturbed by those efforts, as a former
governor of Cochinchina told a French legislative
board of inquiry in 1907: "Some hundred Annamites

speak French, some thousand babble the language . . .
as for the rest of the population, it knows neither
Annamite nor French."[32]   Earlier, in a speech delivered at the competition of scholars at Nam-Định,
Beau had assured everyone that France, "respectful
of human rights, would not injure the soul of the
people of which it had assumed the guardianship."[33]

Vietnamese educators had waited for this liberal
attitude for too long. They filed an official request to open a "free private school along the lines
of the civilizing policy of the Protectorate Government."[34] The permission took two months to arrive
and was received in May 1907. But in the meantime,
the school, enthusiastic over Governor General
Beau's intentions, had already started two classes
for beginners in *quốc ngữ*, the romanized transcrip-
tion of Vietnamese.

The courageous step in adopting quốc ngữ as the
basic language of instruction was nothing but revolutionary. In other contemporary schools it was
either Chinese characters or the French language
which constituted the official vehicle for instruction. Quốc ngữ, invented by a group of European
missionaries in the seventeenth century, was rele-
gated to the instruction of catechism in the missionary schools or taught in government schools merely
as a transitional step toward learning French. In

42

the eyes of the nationalists, quốc ngữ was still
considered in the 1900s as a tool for religious
propaganda, a sort of memorial of shame, and perhaps
a dangerous trap set up by the Western conquerors
for the annexation of Vietnam. A few progressive
scholars, it is true, realizing bitterly the weakness
of both Chinese and its sister chữ nôm,[35] had begun
to adopt quốc ngữ late in the nineteenth century.
They adopted it grudgingly, however, because of its
connection with its Western inventors. In order to
learn it, scholars hid themselves in secluded
places.[36] The scholars at the Đông Kinh, on the
contrary, not only learned quốc ngữ without shame,
but vindicated its use as a universal language of
instruction. The famed Phan Châu Trinh demolished
the tyrannical reign of Chinese in definite terms--
"without the overthrow of the Chinese characters,"
he said, "we cannot save Vietnam."[37]

It took the first scholars much courage to overthrow the pictorial Chinese characters, which for
almost two thousand years had constituted the single
language of instruction in Vietnam. In concrete
terms, this meant they had to break the centuries-
old habit of reading and writing from right to left.
They took up the opposite approach with the romanized
script, which ran "clumsily from left to right like
nothing better than an earthworm." An influential

43

supporter of the Đồng Kinh group, in an article on
the foundation for the development of education, saw
a convincing reason for adopting the new script:
"First and foremost, we must learn quốc ngữ in order
to avoid the discrepancy between the spoken and the
written word."[38] To hesitant people who doubted the
competence of the new script as a modern instrument
of culture, one school textbook lists these practical
advantages:

> All natives going to school should take up
> quốc ngữ as a primary medium, so that even
> women and children can master the language
> within a few months. With quốc ngữ we can
> also record events of the past and the pres-
> ent; and our letter-writing can be carried
> out with both art and accuracy. This is
> indeed the first step toward the develop-
> ment of intelligence.[39]

But it was not mere modernization of the medium
of instruction that Vietnamese scholars wanted when
they took pains to "throw away the beloved brush
for the prosaic steel pen." It was the symbol of a
dramatic drive for universal modernization. A young
scholar led the movement in expressing this new
trend in one of his popular songs:

> (Let's) open new frontiers and turn to new
> learning, Greet this new drive for the build-
> ing of a new nation.[40]

These rhetorical repetitions of *new*, as in New Frontier, "new drive," "new nation," were not exclusive to a single author. Textbooks and written materials in use at the school were filled with evocative terms like *modern education*, *modern newspapers*, *modern literature*, and *modern science*.

To begin this new learning, scholars had to break with the past. Those who did so called themselves enlightened scholars. They regarded themselves as awakening from the deep sleep of an unproductive system of education and rejected the old for the new. And, having said this, they did not hesitate to tear up their old academic degrees; Phan Bội Châu disavowed his enviable degree as number one graduate in a regional contest, and Nguyễn Thượng Hiền and Trần Quý Cấp, their hard-won doctoral degrees from the imperial court at Huế.[41] Others, like Dương Bá Trạc, a Cử-nhân (holder of license) when only seventeen years old denounced his degree with these satirical lines:

> Do you still envy my license?
> I am ready to sell it to you for one penny.[42]

Progressive scholars realized bitterly that, since the coming of the French, traditional exams had too often been scandalously corrupted by blackmail.[43]

The image of the unhappy Tú-Xương (1870-1907), an encyclopedic scholar who was too independent-minded to pass the exams, obsessed all promising students.[44] One significant reform advocated by the Đông Kinh scholars was to liberate the tradition-bound examinations from their petrified forms, while allowing room for productive discussion and original thinking, "so that what the student actually learns and is tested upon is not divorced from what he must do in real life."[45]

Now awakened, progressive scholars wanted their fellows to be the same. They imputed the backwardness of the country and the loss of its independence not only to the degraded system of selecting the elite but also to the mood and attitude of conservative scholars, who in the twentieth century still thought the earth was square, still worshiped the Ancients as infallible masters, and still considered the political doctrine of China's philosophers as immutable wisdom, in contrast to the "shortsighted and mercantile art of Westerners." Worse still, charged the progressives, a number of conservatives never dared to make a ten-mile trip away from home without bitter complaint, frightened as they were by everything new and challenging. They preferred to slumber in eternal lethargy beside old books rife with termites, arguing on behalf of their masters

46

that it was useless to try since any progress lies in the hands of fate.[46]

The Đông Kinh group of educators set out earnestly to overhaul books, both in form and content. To do this, the school was provided with a small and unsophisticated printing shop. The criterion for the selection of material for publication was their modern character. The four books and the five classics, as well as other Confucian apocrypha that were "fit to print" were, in effect, reprinted, but with modern commentaries. The presentation of material was also an innovation. Although wooden fonts were still used for the printing of Chinese characters, the school made every effort to print them neatly and cleanly, thus surpassing the older editions in quality. The paper in use was a local product, the very white and good-looking paper from Bưởi village. And on the opening page of each school textbook there was an illustration in pink. The drawing was realistic, representing a rosy and healthy alert youth supporting the globe with his hands[47]--no small ideal for modern students, indeed!

In addition to books in Chinese characters, a great deal of quốc ngữ literature was also printed, which, together with the Chinese "new" books, was distributed to students or sent free-of-charge to other private schools entertaining similar ideals

47

and programs. These materials were also sold to bookstores without profit. Other materials which the school considered too revolutionary in the eyes of the French were printed in litho and distributed surreptitiously.[48]

The books most in demand were of a popular character like *Quốc-Dân Đọc-Bản* (The People's Primer), *Nam-Quốc Vĩ-Nhân* (The Nation's Great Men), *Việt-Nam Vong-Quốc Sử-Lược* (Short History of Vietnam's Downfall), *Nam-Quốc Địa-Dư* (The Nation's Geography), and *Văn-Minh Tân-Học Sách* (The Manual of Modern Civilization). According to principal Quyền, the *People's Primer* was the most successful book in the school's printing history, with a supply of tens of thousands of copies being exhausted within a nine-month period and with more orders from the nation's bookstores unsatisfied.[49] But the cream of the school's textbooks was, of course, *The Manual of Modern Civilization*, which constituted a sort of manifesto of the school and of the movement it inspired. This book, written by an anonymous educator, begins with some argument showing civilization to be "a value whose price is competition,"[50] then develops into a contrast between old Vietnam and contemporary Vietnam, with emphasis on the ignominious decadence of the latter. The author attributes this decadence to four major factors: ignorance of the world situa-

48

tion, a tragic rejection of foreign technology, superstitious worship of the Ancients, and a feudal respect for the mandarins at the expense of the common people. In the last part of the manual, the author makes six recommendations for the education of the masses: (1) use of quốc ngữ, (2) revision of books to bring them up to date, (3) alteration and improvement of the examination system, (4) promotion of the national elite, (5) development of industry and trade, and (6) promotion of the press.

In addition to printing and publishing books, the Đông Kinh group farsightedly saw the importance of the press to a modern Vietnam. Of the two journals then operating in Tongking, the school owned one, the *Đăng-Cổ Tùng-Báo* edited by Nguyễn Văn Vĩnh, the Đông Kinh French teacher. Later, in winning over Đào Nguyên Phổ, the editor of the other journal the *Đại-Việt Tân-Báo*, the school group secured the viewpoints and shared the services of all the press media then available in the whole of Tongking.[51]

In the school's textbooks and other published materials another recurrent concept was "Western" and "Westernization." This constituted another revolutionary step forward on the part of progressive scholars. Not long before them, Vietnam's famous mandarin-king Tự-Đức (reigned 1847-1883) used to refer to Westerners as "white demons," while admitting

that only the Chinese were civilized people.[52] And
as late as in the 1900s, Westernization, to the vast
majority, still meant nothing more than becoming
"French valets." To crush this inveterate prejudice,
the scholars of the Đông Kinh group resorted to the
prestige of their own academic achievements and
their patriotic records. They, too, were the best
representatives of Eastern culture, but they were
far from despising Western civilization. They did
not spare praise and admiration for France. Students
at the Đông Kinh were encouraged to master the French
language and culture. French classes at the school
were crowded, even though some fee was charged the
students.[53] Phan Châu Trinh was full of admiration
for French democracy and French technology in the
construction of roads and railroads, the repair of
dikes and bridges, and the use of steam power and
telecommunications.[54] He advocated a frank and egalitarian collaboration between the French and the
natives. Toward this goal, the nationalists were to
abandon violence and the French were to carry out
necessary reforms.[55] The school advised its students
in these positive terms:

> Now that the government begins to be
> generous and wants us to imitate the West,
> . . . .
> Now that Great France is willing to open
> our minds, (Let's) intently watch for any

good craft to learn.56

Definitely there is some sting in these lines of
verse praising "Great France," because the necessary
reforms from the French, as demanded by the nationalists, never came. In another poem, an author expressed deep frustration because the work of
modernization thus far had been carried out by French
authoritarian masters with

> The (Vietnamese) King serving as figurehead,
> And his nation doing forced labor.57

The nationalists questioned France's good faith
and sincerity in her civilizing mission to Vietnam.
They resented the French especially for not allowing
them to import liberal Western thinking, of which
they believed France could only be proud. Instead,
French colonialists kept a suspicious eye on every
move by any native suspected of collusion with
foreign powers, including Vietnam's "mother country."
All cultural and educational material from France
was pitilessly pruned of its "demagogic and seditious" character.58 Not many educated Vietnamese
then knew that authors like Montesquieu and Rousseau
were French. Yet, with much skill and cunning, the
Đông Kinh group regularly had a variety of progres-

sive materials smuggled into Vietnam from China and
Japan, in the face of French security agents. Immediate translation was carried out by its translation
pool. Thus, modern terminology such as *economy,*
progress, and *revolution,* fresh from the translators'
pens, appeared in the country for the first time and
was soon assimilated into its common stock of every-
day vocabulary.[59] Not infrequently, the school also
received, in their Chinese versions, copies of
treatises on potentially explosive political and
sociological topics written by French philosophers,
such as *Le Contrat Social* by Rousseau and *l'Esprit*
des Lois by Montesquieu.

If France's image was irremediably injured in
the eyes of the Đông Kinh group, Japan's, on the
contrary, had the unambiguous admiration of the
educators. This great Asian nation had so well
learned the lessons of Western powers that, for the
first time in the world's modern history, Asia had
scored a superb victory over a European power, in the
Russo-Japanese War of 1904-05. Puzzled by Japan's
power and almost disbelieving their eyes, a number
of scholars like Phan Châu Trinh and Trần Quý Cáp
disguised themselves as fruit vendors and boarded a
Russian warship which took refuge in the Cam Ranh Bay
after Admiral Rodjestvensky's fiasco at the battle of
Tsushima Straits.[60] The scholars saw what they

wanted to see: the only successful way for the East
to assert itself against the West was to acquire the
technology of the West.[61] In a very popular song,
"Á-tế-á Ca" (the Asian Epic), distributed by the
school and reportedly known by heart by every school-
child at the time, these lines stood out conspic-
uously like a challenge:

> Japan, a nation of common culture (with us),
> Has been the first to hoist the flag of
> independence;
> In the inauguration of the modern era,
> Who can compete with the Emperor of Japan?[62]

From Japan, the undisputed revolutionary leader
at the time, Phan Bội Châu, from his modest headquarters in Yokohama, led an authentic Vietnamese
"exodus to the East,"[63] which by 1907 numbered no
fewer than 115 self-exiled students.[64] In addition
to his grave responsibilities of financially and
morally supporting the growing number of these
students, Phan Bội Châu also busied himself in con-
versations with prominent Japanese political personages[65] and self-exiled Chinese revolutionaries.[66]
He wrote prolifically to earn a living for his
students and himself and sent his works to the Đồng
Kinh School in Hanoi for dissemination and study.
Thus he kept his progressive scholars and students at
home informed of the most up-to-date developments in

Japan's odyssey to world power. The Đông Kinh group,
when teaching its students Japanese geography and
political history, conveyed to the students the
charismatic image of the "eldest yellow brother."
This, in terms of the Confucian ethics practiced by
the scholars, underlined a "brother-keeper" role
which Japan was to play in Asia.

But, beyond Japan, it was modernization along
the lines of Europe and America that the Đông Kinh
group wanted for Vietnam:

> Our country from time immemorial until
> recently
> Has only slavishly followed China.
> We competed with one another, learning
> merely what is decadent,
> And of Europe and America we know nothing.[67]

With unreserved fervor they made their first
acquaintance, in their translations, with Greek and
Western thinkers like Plato, Socrates, Aristotle,
Bacon, Descartes, Montesquieu, Voltaire, Rousseau,
Darwin, Adam Smith, and Herbert Spencer. With the
same unreserved fervor, they admired such great
figures and statesmen of the West as Washington,
Napoleon, Peter the Great, Mazzini, Garibaldi,
Cavour, Bismarck, and Von Moltke.[68] Advice was
candidly given to Vietnamese girls to marry only
national heroes of the caliber of America's Washing-

ton or the Philippines' Aguinaldo.[69] Self-exiled patriots were almost shocked at the contrast between the stifling tyranny at home and the freedom abroad. They were deeply impressed by the economic vitality and atmosphere of political freedom in British Hongkong. Phan Bội Châu sent a number of his students to study in Hongkong, Thailand, and Germany, also. The aim and goal of this drive for Westernization was thus to build a Vietnam which was educationally progressive, economically prosperous, socially liberal, and politically independent. In brief, it was the bold idea and program to transform Vietnam into a modern Western-type nation that the progressive scholars had in mind.

Of the West, the Đông Kinh scholars envied first and foremost the creative spirit which had opened the gates for unlimited progress in science and technology for Europe and America. From this very spirit of creative thinking, stated the *Manual for Modern Civilization*, stem all the scientific disciplines current in the West, like "acoustics, optics, physics, electricity, mineralogy, hydraulics, aerodynamics, chemistry, geology, astronomy, mathematics and mechanics, and so forth and so on."[70] After mentioning the fact that Asia--not elsewhere-- was the cradle of science, the manual went on to contrast the state of unproductive sterility of the

East with the prestigious versatility in scientific
discovery of such Western minds as Watt and Edison.
Then, qualifying Vietnam's civilization as static and
Western civilization as dynamic, the book found the
profound cause of the West's unlimited progress in
what it called the opposition principle. In Western
institutions, the manual said, "there is at the top
the Congress, which maintains the nation's policies,
and, at the bottom, the press, which vindicates the
will of the people."[71]

The Đông Kinh group also envied the competitive
spirit of the West in trade. Progressive scholars,
unlike their old-fashioned fellows who despised the
"mercantile flair" and the "religion of wealth" of
Westerners, vied with one another in emulating the
West in business enterprises and financial adventures
to better their personal incomes, finance free private schools, and assist Vietnamese students abroad.
Thus, a number of enthusiastic scholars threw away
their traditional brushes for good, to take up
tougher tools like axes and picks to break virgin
land for growing cinnamon, tea, and other "economic"
plants for export. Nguyễn Quyền, the Đông Kinh's
principal, founded a commercial firm of his own.
Phan Châu Trinh founded a commercial company and
owned a cinnamon tree plantation. Other scholars set
up small handicraft factories to manufacture hats,

clothes, feather fans, wooden shoes, or bamboo trays.
Still other scholars traded in Oriental medicine or
old clothes for the financially deprived people.
Several scholars helped push a drive to advertise
the most famous brands of Vietnamese natural silk.
Typical was the edifying example of Nghiêm Xuân
Quang, who, despising his brilliant doctorate which
he had won with flying colors in three successive
competitions and resigning his mandarinal post in
Lạng-Sơn, ventured into the more humble trade of promoting native silk fiber. Still more ambitious
scholars set out to improve the soil and open new
land for plantations, and some even rushed into the
uncertain quest for Tongking's precious ores and
minerals.[72]

In all these financial adventures, a few scholars succeeded and became rich as individuals, but the
vast majority of these projects, because they were
poorly planned and poorly supported by capital, were
doomed to fast failure. Indeed, Vietnam's elite had
a long way to go to match the West's in economic
management and financial genius.

A MOVEMENT OF MASS EDUCATION

> People's rights derive from their enlight-
> enment. France as a republic, America as
> a republic, stem from the enlightenment of
> their subjects; the constitutional regimes
> of Japan, Britain, Germany are also the
> result of their peoples' enlightenment.[73]
> --Phan Bội Chau

The Đồng Kinh group did not want to limit their innovations to their school. In the intention of the
progressive scholars, the movement had to be country-
wide. To them, modernization was inseparable from
mass education, which had been completely ignored
by the French.[74] They saw in the obscurantist attitude of the French a dramatic cause of the people's
ignorance. Phan Châu Trinh, going further, said in
a letter of protest to Governor General Beau in 1906
that ignorance was not his only concern. His principal worry was that under the educational and political regime of the French the natives had become
selfish, morally weak, and uprooted.[75] He saw
another cause for national decay in those who then
collaborated with the French--Vietnam's monarchs and
mandarins. The first nationalist in Vietnam to advocate democracy, Trinh demanded the complete abolition of old-fashioned political institutions and the
establishment of democratic values, in the image of
the French republic. More conservative than Trinh,

58

Phan Bội Châu advocated a reformation of the monarchy by replacing incapable kings and mandarins with
more competent and patriotic ones. But even Châu
abandoned his last monarchist leanings immediately
after the Chinese Revolution of 1911. Both political educators agreed to give top priority to seeking
every means possible to overhaul the old educational
values and develop the nation's intellectual maturity, to revive its patriotic flame, and to enhance
its moral courage for necessary reforms. To achieve
these goals, they resorted to the public media available at the time--study groups, public lectures,
patriotic chants, popular verse, and lullabies. In
short, they used every available method except
violence.[76]

Study groups for discussion and dissemination
of "new" ideas were created. A modern concept of
patriotism was developed, based not on blind allegiance to the kings and mandarins, but on national
solidarity and unreserved devotion to the nation's
heroes. New mottoes and key ideas replaced the old,
for example, "the people being the foundation,
monarchs and mandarins may go, the nation will remain
forever."[77] But in order for the nation to survive
changes were necessary. Reforms in the ways of life
of the common people were loudly demanded, ranging
from the cutting of long hair and fingernails, the

59

cleaning of teeth, the use of soap, and the wearing
of uncomplicated clothing, to more sophisticated
innovations in public relations and national economy.

Public lectures took the form of a real campaign. These lectures were organized usually on the
first and the fifteenth days of the lunar month.
Lectures were not confined to Hanoi citizens. A
number of lecturers traveled the country far and
wide, reaching not only the towns and districts,
but also the villages, in Tongking and Annam. The
most widely known lecturers of the time were Hoàng
Tăng Bí, Trần Tấn Bình, Lương Trúc Đàm, Nguyễn Quyền,
Dương Bá Trạc, Nguyễn Văn Vĩnh, Phan Châu Trinh.
Phan Châu Trinh was the most successful. A true
image maker and breaker, he "toured the country from
north to south, beating the drum to stir up nationalist energies; and incessantly harassing the backward and corrupt mandarins with his sarcastic
verses."[78]

Common subjects were the nation's culture,
religion, and history, and economic and social reform. A typical public lecture performed by the
school group usually began with a reading by the
lecturer of some topical piece taken from the
school's two journals, followed by the speech proper,
and then a question-and-answer period.[79]

No small revolutionary innovation during these

60

public lectures was the arrangement of the audience. Women, "separate but equal," now could sit in rows parallel to the men, usually on the right side of the aisle of the lecture hall. Students, enthusiastic but well disciplined, were seated below the women. Most of the women felt very flattered by these encouraging steps in the promotion of equal rights for them, in a society in which the old motto "a boy means one, a girl means naught" was still heard.

No wonder audiences attending these lectures most often filled the halls to capacity. Not infrequently, some women, stirred by the rhetoric of a patriot, burst into tears. They wept when they heard of the suicides committed by scholars of yore who had felt dishonored by the superiority of the French. At other times, they wept for shame for those scholars who had become French henchmen to oppress their own countrymen.[80] Women not only wept, they also knew how to applaud the eloquent lecturers in their fervor for reform.

The French and their collaborators did not view these public lectures favorably. One day during an emotional harangue by two of the school's young teachers, Lương Trúc Đàm and Dương Bá Trạc, at the Ngọc-Sơn pagoda in downtown Hanoi, French police broke in, arrested the two bold instructors, and

took them to police headquarters for interrogation.
They were released that night but were later summoned to a face-to-face confrontation with the
Resident Superior, himself. To the resident's charge
of disturbing national security (a crime then punishable by death), Dương Bá Trạc replied:

> Since France twenty years ago established a
> protectorate here and assumed the task of
> civilizing our country, she has accomplished
> nothing for the advancement of the people's
> thinking. How can you say we attempt to
> disturb national security when we merely
> stand up to do this task and therefore sup-
> port the government! All we tell people
> is to go "modern," to catch up to Western-
> ers, to promote vocational education for
> our country's welfare; these are therefore
> for the interests of the government, how
> can you say (they are) crimes? Besides,
> two months ago we filed a request to open
> a school and conduct public lectures, and
> upon the government's long silence, we have
> assumed a tacit permission, and not because
> we despised the government's law.81

Thanks to this incident, the school shortly afterward
received an official permit.

Among the most popular songs and didactic lullabies distributed by the school, one must cite the
"Á-tế-á Ca" (the Asian Epic). This exceedingly successful piece of verse, after briefly telling the
story of the invasion of Asia by the West, extolled
the modernization of Japan, condemned the obscurantist policy of the French colonialists, and appealed

to the people to unite to develop modern education, regain political freedom, and build a modern nation along the lines of the Western powers. Because of its inflammatory character, the author of this song, like those of many others distributed by the school, remained anonymous. It was thought wise to hide one's name for fear of French retaliation.

But in spite of French fear and suspicion, the Đông Kinh group actually attacked the French only indirectly. What they wanted most was a country-wide educational awakening for social reform. The group tried hard to rid the Vietnamese mind of the memory of their ignominious defeat by a Western power. The *Manual of Modern Civilization* stated that "the yellow race is in no way inferior to the white race. The reason (for our inferiority) is simply that we cannot develop into forms that we have not seen yet."[82]   Basic notions about the nation's background were put into popular verse form to facilitate dissemination in such songs as "Bài Ca Địa-Dư và Lịch-Sử Nước Nhà" (Song of the Nation's Geography and History). Modern political concepts were also injected into the minds of the masses. In the preface of the best-seller *Quốc-Dân Đọc-Bản* (The People's Primer), the author criticized the long-entrenched scholarly concept of only training the elite, while sorely neglecting the education of the masses. Then the author defined

what he meant in modern thinking by such terms as
society, *nation*, and *people*, with the explicit purpose of teaching the common people "to understand in
general lines the basic principles at work in a
modern nation" and, at the same time, "to encourage
our brave youths to realize national cohesion,
patriotism, and respect for public property."[83]

Successful among the masses, progressive scholars were also extremely popular in their first steps
to promote women's rights. To show their enlighten-
ment, women not only wept during the public lectures,
but also oftentimes became so bold as to challenge
the stronger sex. In a poem describing a reassess-
ment of the relationship between husband and wife,
"Tình Phu-Phụ" (Husband and Wife Relationship), progressive women boasted that if men had their Glad-
stone, their Bismarck, they themselves had their
Joan of Arc and Madame Roland.[84] In another poem,
"Nhắn Chị Em Bạn Gái" (A Word to Fellow Women),
these lines rang harsh in the ears of conservative
scholars:

> Fellow women, do you not know
> That we, the weaker sex, do have large
>   women's rights?
> (Let's) bravely lend our hand to share the
>   burden of our youths,
> And make known the worth of an Asian Woman.
> Shame on them, these white-faced scholars
>   in their decadent manners,
> What is the worth of their degree, their

fame, their pompous honors?85

The women, of course, were only criticizing some scholars, because the more progressive ones had already chosen the path of modernization. Nguyễn Quyền, the school's principal, had long before made known his decisive break with the past in a celebrated symbolic gesture. He invited Phan Châu Trinh one day for a haircut. The reason was given in his popular poem "Phen Này Cắt Tóc Đi Tu" (A Haircut to Become Monks This Time):

> This time, (let's) cut our hair to become
>   monks
> And in our pagoda of Modernization recite
>   the prayers
> for Independence.86

The "pagoda of modernization" mentioned by the principal was none other than the Đông Kinh school, itself. Progressive scholars considered themselves a new race of monks, and, like monks praying for their own perfection, the scholars' business now was to care for the nation's independence. In traditional Vietnam, only monks were allowed to have short haircuts, a drastic symbol of renunciation of self and society. Lay people were supposed to wear their hair long. That was why, even after 1900, Vietnamese men still wore hair buns rolled at the nape of the neck.

Haircutting was considered by most of them a profana-
tion according to the Confucian saying, "Thy body
together with thy hair and skin belong to thy
parents and cannot be disposed of."[87] Applauding
Quyền's and Trinh's example, a good number of
scholars cut off their hair. This "hairbun-murder-
ing movement" spread rapidly over several cities and
towns and reached some of the most tradition-bound
regions of Vietnam. In rural places of the two
provinces of Hà-Tỉnh and Nghệ-An, the birthplace of
Phan Bội Châu, teams of haircutters roamed the roads
leading to major market places. Progressive schol-
ars-turned-barbers and their students would stop any
man having a "pigeon-nest-like" hairbun and politely
request, "I beg you, let me dispose of this bun of
backwardness for you." And, to prevent the victim
from possible protest, the barber set out at once to
do his delicate job while singing a moralizing song:

My left hand holding the comb,
My right hand holding the scissors,
Come on! Come on!

Smoothly we go!
Cut yourself off ignorance,
Cut yourself off backwardness. . .[88]

Ironically, French colonials, who naturally
wore their hair short, appeared to be particularly

displeased by this new style of the Vietnamese
scholars. They suspected some dark plot by the
nationalists and opened an investigation of what
they called *Le Mouvement de la Tonsure* (the haircutting movement).[89] The suspicion of the French
proved to be well-founded, when, carried away by the
momentum of change, a number of the school group and
their sympathizers carried their innovative campaign
into the ticklish area of politics. This occurred
when the French attempted to issue new coins. Rumor
had it that the French were planning to confiscate
all of the country's silver and copper and replace
it with worthless iron. In fact, the new coins *were*
iron. One day, when the school faculty was having a
meeting, a stranger entered the room, a poorly
dressed but energetic-looking scholar. He introduced himself simply as a scholar from Hà-Đông
(Tongking), and, talking about the cunning scheme of
the French to introduce iron coins, he proposed a
boycott. The campaign should start with the modest
idea of distributing a pamphlet in verse, *Thiết Tiền
Ca* (The Song of the Iron Coin), one the strange
scholar had himself composed. The school group agreed
to the scholar's idea and immediately printed three
hundred copies for distribution.

Nobody in the Đông Kinh school had expected that
the small pamphlet by Nguyễn Phan Lãng, as the name

67

of the visiting scholar was later known, would have
such an instantaneous effect. The *Song of the Iron
Coin* had the electrifying effect of producing a chain
reaction of universal refusal to accept and circulate
the coin. Finding that the boycott did not stop
with the arrest of a number of "delinquents," the
French decided to withdraw their coin from circulation.[90]

The Ðồng Kinh group was gratified by the unexpected victory of the coin campaign and by the leading role of the school in it, but a few farsighted
educators saw that the school had become, after this
victory, irremediably suspect in the eyes of French
security agents and that maybe it was doomed.

THE VIOLENT END

No violence! Violence means death: you
who are my fellow men and fellow countrymen, you who really love freedom, I have
one and only gift for you: education.91
                              --Phan Châu Trinh

After an emergency meeting, the French Military
Council, whether because of the iron coin incident
or more convincing evidence, handed down a verdict
that the Đông Kinh Free School was a center of rebel-
lion.92 The school's permit was revoked in December
1907. Together with the closing of the school,
orders were given to the cooperatives and study
groups and to the official organ of the school, the
Đăng Cổ Tùng Báo, to suspend all activities indefi-
nitely. Public lectures were no longer tolerated.
Dissemination and storage of the school's material
and publications were punishable as serious crimes.
The school was searched for seditious material.
None was found. By a matter of happy luck for the
scholars, French security agents could not find
where the school concealed all the implicating material that might have led to conviction, so nobody
was arrested. On the contrary, a number of teachers
like Hoàng Tích Chu, Lương Trúc Đàm, Dương Bá Trạc
and Nguyễn Quyền were highly flattered when decrees
from the Resident Superior reached them, appointing

69

them to higher educational positions. The majority
of them, however, declined the offers, suspecting
some political move on the part of the French to
isolate them from the group.[93]

But the cease-fire did not last long. A chain
of political events in which a number of the school
group got involved occurred a few months after the
closing of the school. The first events occurred
in various provinces in Annam from March to May 1908,
when people by the thousands protested in vast demonstrations against excessive taxation and against
the unpopular corvée.[94] Another precipitating event
was an abortive attempt in June of the same year to
poison the French soldiers stationed in the Hanoi
garrisons, whereby nationalists planned to seize
control of the city. The third event was an unsuccessful invasion led by the famous Hoàng Hoa Thám,
the one the French called the Tiger of Yên-Thế,
into Tongking in 1908 from his autonomous region
of Yên-Thế, which had been grudgingly conceded to
him by the French to isolate him from the rest of
Tongking. Since a number of the Đồng Kinh educators
were involved in this political turmoil, the French
were fast to conclude that the notorious school was
to blame for all the upheavals.[95] Thus, all the
teachers and staff were once again summoned, and a
great number of them were tried and convicted of

"advocating the rights of the common people and plotting with the traitor (meaning Phan Bội Châu) for popular rebellion."[96] Phan Bội Chau, then in Japan, was condemned to death *in absentia*. Phan Châu Trinh, the popular lecturer, was condemned to immediate decapitation but narrowly escaped it through the intervention of a French friend. His death sentence was commuted to detention in Poulo Condore, the notorious island fifty miles off Cochinchina which the French had turned into a concentration camp. Dr. Trần Quý Cáp, a friend of Phan Châu Trinh, was cruelly executed.[97] Others, like Nguyễn Quyền, Lê Đại, Võ Hoành, Ngô Đức Kế, and Dưỡng Bá Trạc, were condemned to hard labor in Poulo Condore. Lương Văn Can, the director, who was released after the interrogations, was later deported to Phnom Penh. Some luckier members or followers either were put under house arrest (Hoàng Tăng Bí) or went into self-imposed exile abroad (Nguyễn Thượng Hiền).[98] The Đông Kinh Free School could no longer survive the storm.

Even if it had not fallen from grace with the French, other causes would have shortened the life of the school. First, this early drive towards modernization had not been carried on in a very scientific spirit. The teaching of sciences was modern only in intent. Lacking interchange with

71

nations pioneering in scientific fields, they only revised old books written under Tự Đức (*Bác Vật Tân Biên*) or even resorted to Chinese manuals written as long ago as the Ming dynasty (*Nông Chính Toàn Thư*). Obsolete books in astronomy (*Quản Khuy Lệ Trắc*) were reprinted together with outdated books of medicine (*Nghiệm Phương Tân Biên*), in which traditional authoritative medicine was interspersed with pure quackery.[99] The qualities prevailing in scientific inquiry, like accuracy and precision, were frequently violated. Not a few authors, carried away by propaganda, put the nation's population--then less than fifteen million--at thirty or forty or even fifty million souls.[100] It was not rare to find in so-called top-notch scientific books of the time such thrilling titles as *Japan Has Been Able to Make Artificial Rain for Ten Miles*. And since in Chinese the character for 1,000 (千) is the same as that for 10 (十), except for one additional stroke, Vietnamese translators did not hesitate to make it *Japan Has Been Able to Produce Artificial Rain for One Thousand Miles!*[101] Although a certain mandarin doctor was reported to have sold all his meager rice-fields to buy electrical devices and chemical equipment in his eagerness to perform scientific experiments, rote memorization was still the rule, not the exception, in learning sciences. "Modern" school

maps, accessories, and other school aids were pur-
chased from second-rate modern powers like Japan or
China. As a substitute for scientific demonstration
and experimentation, young scholars used to copy
intricate lessons in science and mathematics, with
great devotion to calligraphy. Physical education
at first was listed high among the priority subjects, and the school tried hard to equip itself with
an unsophisticated but modern playground. Later,
however, lacking qualified coaches and interest by
the students, it simply fell into disuse.[102]

In addition to shortcomings in modern educational practices, the school had a more serious problem
which endangered its very existence. Conflicts of
views and policy often occurred in the group between
the young and the old, between the West-oriented[103]
and the Asia-oriented, between the nonviolent and
the revolutionaries. But the most serious problem
was to decide which conduct to adopt vis-à-vis the
protectorate government. There was the pacifist
group, which wanted to limit the school's activities
to those strictly educational. The leader of this
camp was Phan Châu Trinh. Then there was the revolutionary group[104] under the leadership of the absent
Phan Bội Châu, which contended that educational and
social modernization were empty unless they first rid
the country of the French.[105] While the advocates of

73

nonviolence devoted their energies to preaching innovations in education and reforms in customs and
manners, the advocates of revolutionary action exploited the very successful campaigns in haircutting,
public lectures, and learning the vernacular to stir
the emotions of the masses for armed and overt rebellion. Thus, physical education, which first figured
in the schedule as an innocent modern subject, was
soon interpreted by the violent group as the first
step in providing the students with training in box-
ing and the use of weapons. Furthermore, the visits
paid by Sun Yat-sen, the leader of the upcoming
Chinese Revolution, to some members of the Đông Kinh
group once or twice in 1907 seemed to encourage the
violent camp to follow the path of the Chinese
revolutionaries.[106]

This internal paradox at one time grew so sharp
that Lương Văn Can, the director, fearing for the
future of the school because of drastic measures
which might be taken by the French, proposed in one
meeting with the staff channeling the two tendencies
into two separate groups. Those favoring nonviolent
reforms would stay with the school, those advocating
armed struggle would join underground forces. The
proposal drew a unanimous vote in favor, but they
did not have time to implement it before the French
took action.[107] This event indicated that the violent

camp, although very influential, was nevertheless a minority in the school.

In spite of its flaws and shortcomings, the Đông Kinh Free School was a unique educational phenomenon in modern Vietnam. Its influences were incalculable. There were cases of countless individual conversions to the cause of the school movement, like that of Đào Nguyên Phổ[2], the famous editor of the *Đại Việt Journal*, a former number one doctoral graduate at the imperial court, who, upon learning of the Đông Kinh drive for reforms, was credited with having rid himself of his opium-smoking habit in a spectacular shattering of his opium kit. This made sensational headlines throughout Tongking, and from then on Dr. Phổ[2]'s important journal made common cause with the school group.

The tremendous impact of the Đông Kinh school can also be seen in the swift establishment of other free private schools in virtually every province of Tongking[108] and in a number of others in Annam. In Tongking, the best known of these institutions were the Mai-Lâm Free School (Hoàng Mai) and the Ngọc-Xuyên Free School (Hàm Long).[109] As for Annam, in the province of Quảng Nam (the birthplace of Phan Châu Trinh), alone, there were three major private schools of the Đông Kinh type, namely, the free schools of Dien Phong, Phuc Binh, and Phuc Lam.[110]

Besides the establishment of educational institutions, the Đông Kinh movement also accounted for the tremendous promotion of quốc-ngữ into being the national language of instruction, as it has been ever since. The curious success of popular pocket-size best sellers written in quốc-ngữ during the period from 1910 to 1916, such as *Hoàng Trừu, Thạch-Sanh, Kim-Vân-Kiều, Cung-Oán Ngâm-Khúc, Trạng Lợn, Trạng Quỳnh,* explained in part the profound linguistic and cultural trend that was taking place under the influence of the Đông Kinh school. It was reported that well-entrenched conservative scholars, finally attracted to the new cause, did not hesitate to trade centuries-old precious books written in Chinese for these five-penny modern short stories in the vernacular.[111] Nevertheless, this battle for the promotion of quốc ngữ was not won without a fierce fight. Later, in talking with some of his friends, Nguyễn Quyền, the former principal, described the problem:

> At the very start, my friends and I spent
> excessive energy and patience winning over
> conservative scholars to believing that
> the vernacular can effectively promote mass
> education and should be adopted as the
> basic language of instruction in
> schools. . . Whereas my friends and I
> stand up in camp of those advocating the
> use of the vernacular as the tool for pop-
> ularizing Western education and for abolish-
> ing once and for all petrified poetry and

old-fashioned literary forms, the *majority* of the scholars stand fast on their front of keeping Chinese and of conducting examinations as of yore.[112]

But, to the credit of the principal of the Đông Kinh and his courageous friends, the battle was, nevertheless, won.

Other evidence of the influence of the Đông Kinh movement was shown through the constructive reaction by the colonial government in accomplishing a number of goals set up by the school. Late in 1907, when the Đông Kinh of the nationalists was in full swing, the French founded a new school in Hanoi named Tân Quy, the short form for Học Quy-Tân Trường, (School for the Learning of Modernization). They appointed a renowned scholar, Nguyễn Tái Tích, as director.[113] Curiously enough, the Tân-Quy also adopted the idea of "vertical education," practiced at the Đông Kinh school, which allowed students of a variety of educational abilities to be grouped under three levels of study under the same roof. Beginners were accepted from thirteen years of age for elementary education. Students up to twenty-four years of age could be accepted for secondary education, and older students up to forty-eight years old could be enrolled for higher education. Clearly, the Tân-Quy was opened to compete with the Đông Kinh.[114]

Like the opening of the Tân-Quy, the opening by
the French of the University of Hanoi, also in 1907,
needed the initiative and stimulation of the Đông
Kinh educators. The French thus far had always
refused to permit the establishment of institutions
of higher learning for education-hungry Vietnamese
youth. Of course, some sort of higher education
was provided by the nationalists in the Đông Kinh,
using Chinese as the second language of instruction
to teach students the so-called three histories
(native, Asian, and Western). But, being short of
resources and qualified staff, the Đông Kinh group
realized that only a state-supported university could
stand squarely on its own feet. Thus, one day three
teachers from the school, Lương Trúc Đàm, Đỗ Chấn
Thiết, and Dương Bá Trạc, sat down and wrote an emotional letter to the Resident Superior of Tongking,
requesting "the abolishment of the old system of
examinations and the immediate opening of a higher
institution for the education of the Vietnamese
elite."[115]

The Đông Kinh group certainly must have found it
unbelievable, when, not very long after that request,
the editor of the *Đại Việt Journal*, himself, leaked
the good news that Governor General Beau had decided
to open a university in Hanoi.[116] The day the university opened its doors, a good number of teachers

from the Đồng Kinh school found the time to attend
its first classes. Their enthusiasm soon gave way
to disappointment. Only one or two among them, like
Phạm Duy Tốn and Nguyễn Văn Vĩnh, who were already
proficient in French, could understand anything of
what the French lecturer said. After the lecture,
one courageous student requested the very honorable
professor to give him some supplementary reading
material to help him understand the lesson. The
Frenchman dismissed him with a large gesture showing
him the library. Shortly after its opening, the
first university of Vietnam under French aegis closed
its doors for "lack of students." Not only frustrated, the nationalists felt deeply that they had
been cheated.[117]

Another French reaction, this time of more
lasting benefit, were the educational reforms of
1908 by the Conseil de Perfectionnement de l'Enseignement Indigene (Council for the Improvement of
Education of Indigenous Persons).[118] The central
ideas of the reforms were the provision of a limited
vertical education, culminating in three years of
secondary education for able natives in the cities,
the adoption of quốc ngữ for elementary and primary
classes, and the introduction of French--only as an
elective subject--in primary classes. Students
enrolled at Franco-vernacular schools numbered about

79

10,000 in 1909. By 1913, the number of students reached 46,000.[119] As for the abolition of the centuries-old examination system advocated by the Đông Kinh group, it was finally carried out in 1915 in Tongking and 1918 in Annam[120] to the satisfaction of those Đông Kinh members who had outlived their sentences in Poulo Condore.

Also in 1908, the Resident Superior in Tongking established a publications commission, which, like the one set up by the Đông Kinh group one year before, was in charge of editing and publishing modern textbooks, but this time, of course, more in tune with colonial policy. Learning from the bitter lesson of the Đông Kinh rebellion, the French took greater pains to stop the insidious infiltration of new ideas from Japan and China. From then on, even a mere primer for Chinese pupils at Chinese schools had to be meticulously scanned and purged of possible "seditious learning" before official use was permitted. Plans were under way for the creation of a scholarship-sponsors association to attract Vietnamese students, not to Japan, but to France. At the same time, more teachers were being trained and more Vietnamese educators were being sought out to collaborate with the French in the production of educational textbooks, including Ngô Giáp Đậu, Trần Văn Thông, Trần Văn Khánh, and the author and ex-viceroy of Tongking Hoàng Cao Khải. The central theme, with regard to civic education, of the French-sponsored publications commission did not vary much from the old line, except that more emphasis was given to French and Vietnamese collaboration. The reason, according to one of the textbooks for children, was simply that Vietnam, a small state bordering on big nations, could not survive without the protection of Great France and could not achieve modernization without the prestige of French education and culture.[121]

Never before in its colonial history had Vietnam witnessed such a great wave of education innovation as that of the post-Đồng Kinh period. It was tragic that the movement culminated in violence, an outcome long cautioned against by farsighted scholars like Phan Châu Trinh. Yet, as paradoxical as it seems, the few months of violence succeeded in bringing about more reforms for Vietnam than more than forty years of obedience and passive submission to the French.

EPILOGUE

HOMAGE TO THE ĐÔNG KINH'S DIRECTOR AT HIS DEATH
(June 13, 1927)

Fellow countrymen:[122]

With the passing away of Lương the patriot,

Our sorrow, far from an individual one, is
country-wide.

I, a laborer without talent,

Want to celebrate sincerely the mourning of our
hero.

O fellow countrymen of a Vietnam sprung from
the Lạc Hồng,[123]

Determined as we are by a collective grief,

Let us commemorate dearly the labors of our
patriot[124]

Who has spent his whole life for our people and
nation.

For scores of years and far and wide in the
country

Together with (Principal) Quyền, he laboriously
worked;

Together with his sons,[125] he spent all his
energies

Inciting the awakening of his fellow countrymen

from their deepest of slumbers.

The heart of the patriot never vacillated

In the midst of the many dangers to which he
     was exposed.

In his efforts to serve as leader of the masses,

His unfailing courage braved all dangers.

The prospect of exile never worried him,[126]

Neither did the parting from his wife and
     children ever sadden his mind.

How great a respect we owe this indomitable
     soul!

His warm teachings still echo in me.

Recalling the Đông Kinh Free School,

My mind is brought to revere this great man

Who, throughout his life's span and with an
     enlightened mind,

Has fulfilled all the duties of a responsible
     citizen.

He told his fellow countrymen to learn from
     Europe and America

. . . .[127]

He redecorated the beauty of the fatherland

By disseminating further our cultural values.

While comparing our nation with others,

We cannot help being ashamed by the progress
     they have made.

Formerly we were possessed of so many great

men and heroes,

Whose names are still recorded in Vietnam's
   history

And whose dedication to the people of this
   country

Incited them to brave dangers and despise their
   lives.

Why, then, do we turn complacent slaves today

And trust other hands for the protection of
   our own selves?

. 128

O friends! With mutual love among fellow
   countrymen,

Let us not forget to continue to bring one
   another to the temple of civilization,

Rid our reputation as well as our body of all
   slavery,

And endeavor to unite within modern associations

So as to make ourselves more enduring than
   other peoples;

This is indeed our people's foremost task.

Fellow countrymen, please do not leave my
   words unheeded.

                    --Chu Văn Tấn, a laborer

84

NOTES

¹Paul Doumer, *L'Indochine Française: Souvenirs* (Paris, 1905), p. 197.

²A proclamation posted on a tree, which was found by the French near Gô-Công in 1862, quoted by Jean Chesneaux in *Contribution à l'Histoire de la Nation Vietnamienne* (Paris, 1955), p. 110.

³The term *nationalist*, hereafter taken as a synonym for *patriot*, is intended to include both those fighting more or less for the restoration of the old order, like Nguyễn Thiện Thuật and Đề Thám, and those whose sense of nationhood was definitely more in keeping with modern times, like Phan Bội Châu and Phan Châu Trinh.

⁴Paul Doumer, *Situations de l'Indo-Chine 1897-1901: Rapport* (Hanoi, 1902), p. 77.

⁵Ibid., p. 126.

⁶Observing a great feat of Western technology, the monumental more-than-a-mile bridge constructed by Doumer in Hanoi, Vietnamese peasants could only show disquiet about the fate of "the dragon at the bottom of the river," now greatly disturbed by the engineering skill of the white man. As to Doumer's highways, they only provoked children's astonishment and caused adults to swear at Westerners for being reckless in their driving like "demigods in their flying chariots." Paul Mus, *Vietnam: Sociologie d'une Guerre* (Paris, 1952), p. 127.

⁷Doumer, *Situations de l'Indo-Chine*, p. 102.

⁸Quoted by Paul Isoart, *Le Phenomène National Vietnamien* (Paris, 1961), p. 211.

⁹The term *scholars* here refers to Vietnam's intellectual elite trained under Confucian discipline up to the time of the abolition of the mandarinal examinations by the French in 1918.

¹⁰The real father of "associationism" as colonial policy in Indochina was not Beau, but Paul Bert, Resident General in Tongking and Annam from February to November 1886, a former French minister of

education. See Thomas E. Ennis, *French Policy and Developments in Indochina* (Chicago: University of Chicago Press, 1936), p. 98 *et seq.*

[11]The Đông Kinh group, it is true, was not the first to advocate the modernization of Vietnam. At the very dawn of the violent confrontation between Vietnam and West, with the resultant defeat of Vietnam, voices advocating modernization as a means to national liberation were heard now and then, among them Nguyễn Trường Tộ, Nguyễn Hiệp, Lê Đỉnh, Phan Liêm, Đinh Văn Điền. But these voices, individual, sporadic, and ignored by both the nation and the court, had no influence on events and no followers. Lê Thành Khôi, *Le Viet-Nam: Histoire et Civilisation* (Paris, 1955), pp. 364-65.

[12]Quoted by Chesneaux, *Contribution à l'Histoire,* p. 185.

[13]See Ibid., p. 187; Nguyễn Hiến Lê, *Đông-Kinh Nghĩa-Thục* (Saigon, 1956), p. 30; Đặng Thái Mai, *Văn Thơ Cách-Mạng Việt-Nam Đầu Thế-Kỷ Thứ XX* (Hanoi, 1964), pp. 57-58.

[14]See Nguyễn Hiến Lê, *Đông-Kinh Nghĩa-Thục,* p. 37; Nguyễn Văn Thái and Nguyễn Văn Mừng, *A Short History of Vietnam* (Saigon, 1958), p. 309; Joseph Buttinger, *Viet-Nam: A Dragon Embattled* (New York: Praeger, 1967), p. 52.

[15]The *Keio Gijuku* has since become the elite Keio University.

[16]An old-time nationalist and a Japan enthusiast, Tăng Bạt Hổ had volunteered to serve in the Japanese navy and participated in the Russo-Japanese War in 1904-05, being decorated several times. Fairly well known at the Japanese court, he was invited to an imperial banquet celebrating Japan's victory over Russia at Port Arthur. It was reported that Ho, moved by Emperor Mutsuhito's kind regards and driven by homesickness, burst out crying in the course of the banquet. It was he who accompanied Phan Bội Châu to Japan in 1905 and introduced him to several Japanese political personages. See Nguyễn Hiến Lê, *Đông-Kinh Nghĩa-Thục*, 2d ed. (Saigon, 1968), pp. 29-32.

[17]*Đông-Kinh* certainly does not mean Tongking, as several Western authors have suggested. The term may only mean Hanoi or Tokyo. Although a number of writers, among then Nguyễn Hiến Lê (ibid., p. 44),

claim that it refers to Hanoi, I disagree for two reasons: (1) in official documents, *Đông-Kinh* had ceased to designate Hanoi since the seventeenth century; and (2) viewing the enthusiasm of all the school's founders for Japan, it is only natural that it meant Tokyo to them.

[18]Buttinger, *Viet-Nam*, p. 152, writes about the school's leaders: ". . . a movement to modernize education led by Phan Châu Trinh, for the Free School of Tongking under Nguyễn Thượng Hiền." In other places he mentions Nguyễn Hiền as principal of the school. All Vietnamese sources indicate that neither Nguyễn Hiền nor Nguyễn Thượng Hiền was the school's principal.

[19]Headed by Vũ Trác, Hoàng Tịch Phụng.

[20]Phan Đình Đôi.

[21]Trần Đình Đức.

[22]Phan Huy Thịnh, Nguyễn Văn Vĩnh.

[23]Miss Nam and Miss Hai. For details, see Nguyễn Hiến Lê, *Đông Kinh Nghĩa Thục*, pp. 55-59; Thanh-Lãng, *Bảng Lược-Đồ Văn-Học Việt-Nam* (Saigon, 1967), pp. 85-86.

[24]Đặng Thái Mai, *Văn Thơ Cách-Mạng*, pp. 58-60; Phạm Văn Sơn, *Việt-Nam Cách Mạng Cận Sử (1885-1914)* (Saigon, 1963), p. 383 *et seq.*

[25]Nguyễn Hiến Lê, *Đông-Kinh Nghĩa-Thục*, pp. 52-53.

[26]Đặng Thái Mai, *Văn Thơ Cách-Mạng*, pp. 57-58.

[27]Phạm Văn Sơn, *Việt-Nam*, p. 384.

[28]Nguyễn Hiến Lê, *Đông Kinh Nghĩa-Thục*, p. 94.

[29]In Đặng Thái Mai, *Văn Thơ Cách-Mạng*, p. 66.

[30]From a speech at the High Council of Indochina, August 28, 1904, quoted in Đặng Thái Mai, *Văn Thơ Cách-Mạng*, pp. 63-64.

[31]J. S. Furnivall wrote about the progress of education in Indochina in this period: "Nowhere in the Tropical Far East was the educational system so keenly criticized at the beginning of the century as in Indo-China. It was blamed both for what it had

done and for what it had left undone." *Educational Progress in Southeast Asia* (New York: Institute of Pacific Relations, 1943), p. 81.

[32]Quoted by Jean Ajalbert, *Les Nuages sur l'Indo-Chine* (Paris, 1913), p. 33; see also Chesneaux, *Contribution à l'Histoire,* p. 197.

[33]Andre Masson, *Histoire de l'Indochina* (Paris, 1950), p. 99.

[34]Đặng Thái Mai, *Văn Thơ Cách-Mạng,* p. 59; for this nationwide demand for more schools, see Phan Khoang, *Việt-Nam Pháp-Thuộc Sử 1884-1945* (Saigon, 1961), p. 460; Hoàng Văn Chi, *From Colonialism to Communism* (New Delhi, 1964), p. 12.

[35]A complex hybrid of semantic and phonetic adaptations of Chinese characters, *chữ-nom,* though it appeared as early as the thirteenth century A.D., was never popular. See Đào Duy Anh, *Việt-Nam Văn Hóa Sử-Cương* (Saigon, 1938), p. 269.

[36]Đàm Xuân Thiều, Trần Trọng San, *Việt-văn Đọc Bản Lớp Đệ Nhì* (Saigon, 1962), pp. 253-55.

[37]Quoted by Thiêu Sơn, *Phổ Thông* 86 (August 15, 1962):11.

[38]Nguyễn Phan Lãng, quoted by Đặng Thái Mai, *Văn Thơ Cách-Mạng,* p. 61.

[39]*Văn-Minh Tân-Học Sách,* quoted by Đặng Thái Mai, ibid., p. 168.

[40]Nguyễn Phan Lãng, "Thiết Tiền Ca," quoted by Tô Trung, *Nghiên-Cứu Lịch-Sử* 29 (August, 1961):55.

[41]Phạm Văn Sơn, *Việtnam,* p. 392.

[42]Nguyễn Hiến Lê, *Đông-Kinh Nghĩa-Thục,* p. 37.

[43]See Đặng Thái Mai, *Văn Thơ Cách-Mạng,* pp. 26-27.

[44]Phạm Văn Diêu, *Việt-Nam Văn-Học Giảng-Bình* (Saigon, 1961), p. 220.

[45]*Văn-Minh Tân-Học Sách;* see Đặng Thái Mai, *Văn Thơ Cách-Mạng,* pp. 172-73.

[46]"Cáo hủ lậu văn"; see ibid., pp. 254-58.

[47] Ibid., pp. 74-75.

[48] Ibid., pp. 58-59.

[49] Đào Trinh Nhất, *Đông-Kinh Nghĩa-Thục*, quoted by Đặng Thái Mai, ibid., pp. 75-76.

[50] In Đặng Thái Mai, *Văn Thơ Cách-Mạng*, p. 160.

[51] See Phạm Văn Sơn, *Việtnam*, p. 384, and Tân Fong Hiệb, *Bách-Khoa*, 32 (May 1, 1958):43-56.

[52] Dương Quảng Hàm, *Việt-Nam Văn-Học Sử-Yếu* (Saigon, 1960), p. 328.

[53] Nguyễn Hiến Lê, *Đông-Kinh Nghĩa-Thục*, p. 40.

[54] Letter to Governor General Beau (August 15, 1906), quoted in Đặng Thái Mai, *Văn Thơ Cách-Mạng*, pp. 188-89.

[55] In contrast with Phan Bội Châu, Trinh was also noted for his suspicion of Japanese intentions and his aversion to foreign aid. See Thế Nguyên, *Phan Châu Trinh*, 2d ed. (Saigon, 1956), p. 32.

[56] Quoted by Nguyễn Ánh, *Nghiên-Cứu Lịch-Sử* 32 (November, 1961):46.

[57] "Á-Tế-Á Ca," quoted in Đặng Thái Mai, *Văn Thơ Cách-Mạng*, p. 268.

[58] "Chapters dealing with the French Revolution of 1789 were glossed over in the programme of French history taught to Vietnamese children." Hoàng Văn Chi, *From Colonialism to Communism*, p. 12.

[59] Phạm Văn Sơn, *Việtnam*, p. 387.

[60] See Nguyễn Phút Tân, *A Modern History of Viet-Nam 1802-1954* (Saigon, 1964), p. 339.

[61] See Đao Văn Hội, *Ba Nhà Chí-Sĩ Họ Phan* (Saigon, 1957), p. 59. In a pamphlet disseminated to discourage parents from sending their children to French schools, a scholar wrote: "For more than twenty years prior to 1903, France intended to seize Annam and make it a colony. She employed in this undertaking all the means possible in order to weaken us and destroy us. At this time, we did not know liberty. We were not aware of the great forces working in civilization. We were ignorant of other peoples. We knew little of oceans and continents.

We dozed in the deepest of slumbers. Today we are awake. We are disturbed by the formidable movements which are rolling over the Far East. This movement is the Russo-Japanese War in which victory has gone to the stronger. Since then, we have directed our footsteps toward Japan, in the hope that by so doing independence would follow." In *L'Asie Française,* May 1913, pp. 218-23, quoted in Ennis, *French Policy,* p. 181.

[62] In Đặng Thai Mai, *Văn Thơ Cách-Mạng,* p. 263.

[63] See Hoàng Văn Chi, *From Colonialism to Communism,* p. 13.

[64] Nguyễn Văn Hầu, *Bách-Khoa* 124 (March 1, 1962): 10.

[65] Among them were Ki (Tsuyoshi) Inukai (1885-1932), journalist and statesman, and a member of the first house of representatives in the Imperial Diet; and Count Shigenobu Okuma (1883-1922), the founder and president of Waseda University in Tokyo. Both men were then key figures in the Progressive party.

[66] The most prominent were Liang Ch'i-ch'ao (1872-1929), scholar and revolutionary leader, founder of the Harmony party; K'ang Yu-wei (1858-1927), Chinese "modern sage" and monarchist reformer; and Sun Yat-sen (1866-1925), the "father of the Chinese Revolution."

[67] In Đặng Thai Mai, *Văn Thơ Cách-Mạng,* p. 62.

[68] Ibid., p. 31.

[69] In "Nhắn Chị Em Bạn Gái," quoted by Đặng Thai Mai, *Văn Thơ Cách-Mạng,* p. 289.

[70] In Đặng Thai Mai, *Văn Thơ Cách-Mạng,* p. 160.

[71] Ibid., p. 163.

[72] See Nguyễn Hiến Lê, *Đông-Kinh Nghĩa-Thục,* pp. 74, 76, 80-82, 93; Phạm Văn Sơn, *Việt-Nam,* 420 n.

[73] *Việt-Nam Quốc-Sử Khảo,* quoted by Lê Sỹ Thắng, *Nghiên-Cứu Lịch-Sử* 104 (November 1967):24.

[74] "The problem of mass education was totally untouched," wrote Virginia Thompson; see *French Indo-*

China (New York: Macmillan, 1937), p. 286.

[75]In Đặng Thai Mai, *Văn Thơ Cách-Mạng*, pp. 198-99.

[76]Expressly condemned by Phan Châu Trinh, violence was nevertheless included in Phan Bội Châu's arsenal of political weapons. However, even Châu, in 1907, advocated a delay in the use of force against the French. See Thế Nguyên, *Phan Bội Châu: Thân-Thế Và Thi-Văn*, 2d ed. (Saigon, 1956), p. 22.

[77]Lê Thành Khôi, *Le Việt-Nam*, p. 392.

[78]Ibid., p. 391, quoted and translated by Buttinger, *Viet-Nam*, p. 51. Trinh's popular image of a young and dynamic, progressive scholar clad in Western-style clothes, hat, and shoes made of handsome local materials caused a whole generation of enthusiastic youths to ape him in the so-called Tây-Hồ fashion. Tây-Hồ was Trinh's alias. See Nguyễn Hiến Lê, *Đông-Kinh Nghĩa-Thục*, p. 62.

[79]Phạm Văn Sơn, *Việt-Nam*, pp. 383-85.

[80]See Nguyễn Hiến Lê, *Đong-Kinh Nghĩa-Thục*, pp. 56, 58, 59.

[81]Ibid., p. 55.

[82]*Văn-Minh Tân-Học Sách*, quoted by Đặng Việt Thanh, *Nghiên-Cứu Lịch-Sử* 25 (April 1961):17.

[83]In Đặng Thai Mai, *Văn Thơ Cách-Mạng*, p. 76.

[84]Ibid., p. 290.

[85]Ibid., p. 289.

[86]Ibid., p. 260.

[87]Quoted by Phạm Văn Sơn, *Việt-Nam*, p. 396.

[88]In Nguyễn Hiến Lê, *Đông-Kinh Nghĩa-Thục*, p. 60.

[89]See Đặng Thai Mai, *Văn Thơ Cách-Mạng*, p. 55.

[90]See Nguyễn Hiến Lê, *Đông-Kinh Nghĩa-Thục*, pp. 50-51.

[91]Quoted by Nguyễn Hiến Lê, ibid., p. 99 n.

[92]Phạm Văn Sơn, *Việt-Nam*, p. 386.

[93]Nguyễn Hiến Lê, *Đông-Kinh Nghĩa-Thục*, p. 93.

[94]Forced labor required from all native adults.

[95]Phan Châu Trinh later told the French the profound cause of the political turmoil of 1908: "The education we have looked for has been denied. . . The people of Annam wish to be educated; they wish to be respected. They desire gradually to obtain their independence. The day when the people of Annam receive their freedom, they will become the friend and ally of the French. Your interests should point out to you the path to be taken. You should accord the Annamites what is right, the reforms they demand." In *L'Asie Française*, May 1913, pp. 218-23, quoted by Ennis, *French Policy*, p. 180.

[96]Phạm Văn Sơn, *Việt-Nam*, p. 431.

[97]This ill-fated scholar, who received his mandarinal doctorate when he was forty years old, was government superintendent of education in the province of Khánh-Hoà. His activities were closely watched over, when, in one of his letters to a friend that was intercepted by the government, he expressed "delight" at the news of popular demonstrations against excessive taxes. The evidence of his "guilt" was reinforced by a sudden search of his house in which a world map and one copy of Phan Bội Châu's *Hải Ngoại Huyết Thư* (Letter Written in Blood from Overseas) were found. His subsequent condemnation read: "With a map of the world hanging on the wall, what is he up to? With a copy of *Letter Written in Blood from Overseas* concealed in a trunk, his (dark) purpose is all the clearer. Although his treachery is not yet translated in external act, premeditation has been committed within his heart. Therefore, he shall be executed 'with his back cut in two' in order to admonish those who plot treason in the future . . . ." See Hồng Liên Lê Xuân Giáo, *Văn-Hóa Nguyệt-San* 13 (November 1964):1483-88.

[98]See details in Phạm Văn Sơn, *Việt-Nam*, p. 388; Nguyễn Hiến Lê, *Đông-Kinh Nghĩa-Thục*, pp. 95-98, 117; Lê Thành Khôi, *Le Việtnam*, p. 392; Chesneaux, *Contribution à' l'Histoire*, pp. 187-88.

[99]See Đặng Thai Mai, *Văn Thơ Cách-Mạng*, p. 88.

[100]See Nguyễn Hiến Lê, *Đông-Kinh Nghĩa-Thục*, p. 50; Đặng Thai Mai, *Văn Thơ Cách-Mạng*, p. 134.

[101] Đặng Thai Mai, *Văn Thơ Cách-Mạng*, p. 88.

[102] See Nguyễn Hiến Lê, *Đông-Kinh Nghĩa-Thục*, p. 41.

[103] Noted Western-oriented scholars were Nguyễn Văn Vĩnh, Phạm Duy Tốn, Nguyễn Bá Học, Trần Đình Đức, Bùi Anh Tạ, and Phạm Đình Dôi.

[104] The most prominent among them were Võ Hoàng, Nguyễn Tung Huong, Đỗ Chấn Thiết, and the three Lường brothers (Lường Trúc Đàm, Lường Nghị Khanh, and Lường Ngọc Quyển). See Nguyễn Hiến Lê, *Đông-Kinh Nghĩa-Thục*, pp. 85-90.

[105] Phan Bội Chau was exceedingly edified by a passage in a biography of Mazzini by Liang Ch'i-ch'ao in which the Italian hero and statesman expressed the need to pursue education and violence simultaneously (see Phạm Văn Sơn, *Việt-Nam*, p. 362 n). At only one time in Châu's life, the French succeeded in luring him into celebrating the philosophy of Franco-Vietnamese collaboration. In a book written in 1918, *Pháp-Việt Đề Huề Chính Kiến Thư* (Political Viewpoints on Franco-Vietnamese Collaboration), Phan Bội Châu extolled the principle of a frank and egalitarian cooperation. But, finding that the French only offered the Vietnamese a collaboration of the type existing between "the horse and the horse-rider," Châu always refused cooperation. When finally caught in 1925, he was offered the highest post the French had ever proposed to a Vietnamese, as Minister of Education. Phan Bội Châu rejected it, preferring to live the rest of his life as a staunch and incorruptible political prisoner under house arrest (see Thế Nguyên, *Phan Bội Châu*, p. 55 *et. seq.*).

[106] See Chương Thâu, *Nghiên-Cứu Lịch-Sử* 91 (October 1966):25.

[107] Nguyễn Hiến Lê, *Đông-Kinh Nghĩa-Thục*, p. 90.

[108] The most noted provinces were Hà-Đông, Bắc-Ninh, Sơn-Tây, Phúc-Yên, Hưng-Yên, Hải-Dương, and Nam-Định. See Nguyễn Anh, *Nghiên-Cứu Lịch-Sử* 102 (September 1967):51.

[109] See Phạm Văn Sơn, *Việt-Nam*, p. 385.

[110] The Dien-Phong school was headed by Phan Thuc Duyen, the Phuc-Binh by Tran Hoanh, and the Phuc-Lam by Le Co. See Nguyễn Anh, *Nghiên-Cứu Lịch-Sử* 102

(September 1967):51, p. 420 n; Dr. Hoàng Ngọc Thành in his doctoral dissertation, "The Social and Political Development of Việt-Nam As Seen Through the Modern Novel" (University of Hawaii, 1968), p. 102, mentions schools of the Đông-Kinh type in Saigon. However, he does not provide the source.

[111]In Đặng Thai Mai, *Văn Thơ Cách-Mạng*, pp. 99-100.

[112]Ibid., p. 61.

[113]Brother of Nguyễn Khắc Hiếu, the first "modern" and most popular poet in colonial Vietnam.

[114]Nguyễn Anh, *Nghiên-Cứu Lịch-Sử*, p. 46; Đặng Thai Mai, *Văn Thơ Cách-Mạng*, p. 65.

[115]Quoted by Nguyễn Hiến Lê, *Đông-Kinh Nghĩa-Thục*, pp. 64-68.

[116]Calling the new institution Indochinese University, the French conceded that this was one of the "reforms imposed upon by the vigor of the national drive" and that it was closed down because the students "showed themselves active propagandists" (Jean Chesneaux, *Contribution à l'Histoire*, p. 190). Another French author, however, maintains that the students at the university did not "in any case" participate in the turmoil (see Isoart, *Le Phenomène*, p. 292). At any rate, the official reason for the shutting down was "lack of students."

[117]See Nguyễn Hiến Lê, *Đông-Kinh Nghĩa-Thục*, pp. 65-68.

[118]Founded by Governor General Beau's decree dated March 8, 1906, the council did not do anything concrete until 1908. See Đào Duy Anh, op. cit., p. 260, and also A. Rivoalen, "L'Oeuvre Française d'Enseignement au Viet-Nam," *France-Asie*, 125-27 (October, November, December 1956):402. One could never exaggerate the part played by the Đông-Kinh group in extorting from Beau what historians called his "reluctant liberalism" and in helping him silence the noisy army of French colonials who were fiercely opposed to any scheme of modernizing the education of the natives.

[119]See Chesneaux, *Contribution à l'Histoire*, p. 196.

[120]See Đào Duy Anh, *Việt-Nam*, pp. 260-62.

[121]See Đặng Thai Mai, *Văn Thơ Cách-Mạng*, p. 100.

[122]A popular piece of verse published in *Đông-Pháp* Journal, June 24, 1927, quoted by Nguyễn Hiến Lê, *Đông-Kinh Nghĩa-Thục*, pp. 169-71.

[123]Thought to be the first rulers of prehistoric Vietnam.

[124]The journal, in another passage, proposed to set aside the following Sunday as a national holiday for the commemoration.

[125]Lương Văn Can had five sons; all of them died on or before reaching the age of thirty, two of them for the revolutionary cause (Lương Nghị Khanh and Lương Ngọc Quyến).

[126]Lương Văn Can was deported by the French to Phnom Penh in 1914, where he reamined until 1924.

[127]Three lines are missing, probably censored by the protectorate government.

[128]Eight lines are missing, probably censored.

ALEXANDRE VARENNE AND
POLITICS IN INDOCHINA, 1925-1926

By William H. Frederick

French Indochina in 1925 was not the victim of colonial indecision or policy fluctuation, but rather
of stagnation and isolation. It is true that between 1886 and 1926 Indochina saw fifty-two changes
in its top administrative post;[1] it is also true that
many of the men who filled that post spent much of
their time undoing the work of their predecessors.
But there was always the same vague goal of making
Indochina the shining point from which French culture
could be beamed to the Far East. And there were
always the same problems: financial imbalance;
social ills caused primarily by Western influence;
corruption in the French administration; and the disruptive pressures and interests of French colonials,
who opposed metropolitan meddling in Indochina, the
inclusion of Vietnamese in higher economic, cultural,
and political affairs, and liberal thinking of any
variety. Although there were hopes of effective
reform under the Governors General Sarraut (1911-14)
and 1917-19) and Long (1920 and 1921-22), these and
other men were able to make little progress in chang-

ing the structure and attitudes of French colonialism. The relatively serious disturbances of 1908
and 1913 were met with severe repression and few
effective efforts at making the sort of changes which
might prevent further occurrences. Paris showed
remarkable ignorance of and disinterest toward Indochina at most times and, until the first cable connection was made in 1922, remained separated from
her colony by thirty days or more of ocean travel.
Inspectors from the Ministry of Colonies were seldom
called upon to perform their function of reporting
on colonial conditions in an objective manner.

Of the valuable coastal regions known today as
North and South Vietnam, Annam and Tongking were
ruled indirectly as protectorates through the imperial
court at Hue and its mandarinate, while Cochinchina,
centered on the Mekong Delta, was treated as a colony
under direct rule. Terminology aside, there was in
fact little difference between the two systems.[2]
Protectorate or colony, the French were clearly
dominant; theirs was the power to legislate and
administrate, and administrative ends were identical,
whether reached by Vietnamese or French officials.
Appointed by the Minister of Colonies, the governor
general of Indochina held in combination most of the
powers of the ministers in the French cabinet.
Under this broad authority, he could suspend all

local councils if he deemed it necessary; in almost
all facets of colonial life he ruled by personal
decree, with the approval of Paris.[3] He was assisted
by the Council of Government, an advisory body meeting once a year in Hanoi and consisting mostly of
high-ranking French functionaries.[4]

Although the governor general had power over
the entire political federation known as the Indochinese Union,[5] he was represented in Cochinchina by
an administration which was entirely French and
imitative of the union in structure. It was headed
by a governor, who was assisted by a privy council
and a colonial council. There were also chambers of
agriculture and commerce, advisory bodies which to
a large extent controlled the economic life of the
colony and which were influential in setting the
direction and degree of its economic development.[6]
The councils, and to some extent the chambers, were
intended to be representative in a limited sense,
but through procedural intricacies all power rested
in the hands of the governor.[7]

The highly centralized administrative system[8]
met very nicely the needs of French capitalists, who
began to take interest in Indochina around 1912 and
rushed there following the Marseilles Exposition of
1922, which featured an Indochina exhibit focused on
investment possibilities.[9] The principal requisites

98

for these capitalists were stability, protection
by, but no intervention from, the government, and
monopoly privileges. Particularly since French tax-
payers felt that the territories should stand on
their own financial feet, the government was not
unwilling to continue the existing system, with its
emphasis on calm, and to make additional provisions
to assure businessmen of security and profits.
French manufacturers were granted monopolies in
Indochinese markets, and no foreign capital except
French was allowed to enter.[10] In 1914, the total
French investment in Indochina was estimated at 500
million francs. Between the years 1924 and 1930,
nearly three billion francs were poured into the
territories, most of them controlled by a relatively
small number of French industrial and banking concerns.[11] Cochinchina became known as the "game preserve" of a handful of capitalists.[12]

Administrators and capitalists alike considered
public politics both unnecessary and undesirable.[13]
In the protectorates, elections and political groups
or movements did not and could not exist legally.
In Cochinchina, residence of the majority of French
in Indochina, elections were held for positions on
the Colonial Council and for the post of deputy to
the Chamber of Deputies in Paris. But the franchise
was limited to French citizens, born or naturalized,

and the number of registered voters was small. In 1928 there were 4,937 voters on the rolls, of whom 2,837 voted in the elections of that year. The deputy was sent to Paris on the strength of 1,130 votes,[14] 80 percent of which were cast by government employees, if the election figures of 1925 are a reliable guide.[15]

Although there were elections in Cochinchina, there was little legal public political activity, and none that was not subject to government control. A Constitutionalist party was founded by several Vietnamese intellectuals in 1923 and permitted to exist, but it was kept under close watch by the government.[16] Fear of political change of almost any nature was rife, and the names *communist* and *Bolshevik* were applied, often indiscriminately and always with effect on those whom the government wished to silence.[17] To speak about a constitution or constitutional rights "was to render oneself immediately suspect. The shadow of the Sûreté (*a police organization*) hung over everything."[18] André Malraux was led to remark in 1925 that "Cochin-China is the only French territory where it is forbidden . . to profess republicanism."[19] He may have been misinformed regarding other French possessions, but Malraux was accurate when he spoke of the political restrictions in Cochinchina.

If Indochina was, in the 1920s, a "political backwater,"[20] it was in some respects intellectually and socially stagnant, as well. As the economic boom reached its peak in 1925-26, the brutalities and boldness of European rule diminished under the influence of more calculating and conservative administrative and financial interests.[21] Whether they did so with approval or not, most contemporary observers saw French society in Indochina as comparable to that in the small-town bourgeois communities of France--rank-conscious, proud, and anti-intellectual. Out of contact with the Vietnamese[22] and separated from Europe and things European,[23] Frenchmen who lived very long in Indochina often became empty, narrow-minded members of a colonial task force; in a sense they "lost Europe but gained nothing in exchange."[24]

Colonials were cognizant of their independent position and strove to keep the prerogatives in authority which they held. On a number of colonial issues administrators and capitalists had their differences, but in regard to indigene policy "they constituted a veritable bloc."[25] Associationist policies were mouthed from time to time after 1908, but assimilationist attitudes were too strong to be easily abandoned, and they remained in force throughout the period before World War II.[26] The ideals of

assimilation were perhaps praiseworthy, but in practice the policy was less admirable and had only
limited application. Vietnamese schoolchildren
began their history lessons with "Our ancestors, the
Gauls . . . ," and Governor General Sarraut said
that "the Vietnamese will receive French culture and
we will accept the consequences,"[27] but the colonial
government kept a tight line on education. The
University of Hanoi, founded in 1907 by Governor
General Beau, was closed the year after because of
the threat of rebellion and not opened again until
1918.[28] Before World War II, the university rarely
had more than five hundred students,[29] and in the
years 1925 and 1926 there was a total of only thirty-
four Bachelors of Arts graduated.[30] Industrial
schools fared not much better, for in the eleven
such institutions in Indochina there were only 1,091
students in 1923.[31] As for education in France itself, it was extremely difficult to acquire the
necessary permission to leave Indochina and even more
difficult to gain entrance to the mother country for
schooling.

Despite their limitations, however, assimilationist policies in Indochina had succeeded by the 1920s
in producing a small number of Vietnamese intellectuals. These men were academically trained in
Western methods and were well-acquainted with

Western--especially French--thought and behavior. A
number of them were even naturalized French citizens.
Nearly all of the intellectuals were frustrated with
both the decayed state of traditional Vietnamese
life and the heavy-handedness of the French colonial
regime, and they sought ways of improving the situations they found objectionable. Lacking real power,
they could only express their opinions and hope thus
to pressure French authorities into action.

In order to sample the thinking of the new
Westernized Vietnamese intellectuals and perhaps to
permit them to expend energy without harmful incident, the liberal-minded Sarraut had encouraged the
growth of the native press.[32] Most of the writing
was done in French and not in *quốc-ngữ*, the romanized
Vietnamese. Newspapers run by Vietnamese were few,
and the government had methods of keeping a rein on
their contents, but officials were disturbed to find
discontent so broadly expressed in the budding native
press that it could be silenced only by closing down
the newly legalized publications. Particularly in
Cochinchina, where the press was relatively free,[33]
expression of Vietnamese opinion led to bitter opposition from French colonials, whose own journalism
was not only violent and personal in its attacks,
but more often than not illegally supported and controlled by the government.[34] Franco-Vietnamese

103

tensions were thus legally brought out into the open
for the first time, and, with no apparent method of
resolving them satisfactorily, they threatened to
bring serious difficulties to the colonial system in
Indochina.

Perhaps because of nearby China's revolutionary
experiences and the French colonial troubles in
Morocco and Syria, both Paris and local colonials
were sensitive to Indochina's restiveness. When
Governor General Martial Merlin narrowly escaped
being killed by a bomb in Canton in 1924 and when
his would-be assassin, a Vietnamese student named
Phạm Hồng Thái, was made a national hero,[35] responsible opinion held that special efforts should be
made to bring the situation under control. French
colonials in Indochina expected that Acting Governor
General Monguillot, who was not inclined to meddle
in local affairs and who was thought to share the
colonials' fears of disorder, would be asked to
continue as the official appointee. In Paris,
Sarraut, who had served twice before as governor
general of Indochina, was thought to be Merlin's
logical successor.[36] But because of a change in the
French government and the electoral victory of the
united leftist parties, known as the Cartel des
Gauches, Alexandre Varenne, a staunch Socialist, was
appointed governor general toward the end of July

1925. It was the first time that a member of the
Socialist party had ever held such a position in the
French Empire.[37]

It is unclear whether the new Painlevé government was unsure of its own first steps or was merely
wary of public opinion, but in any case Merlin was
given the title of Honorary Governor General *in
absentia,* and Varenne's appointment was very clearly
stated to be temporary.[38] Varenne himself was a
cautious choice, being a model of respectability
with a distinguished political record. First elected
to the Chamber of Deputies from his district of Puy
de Dôme in 1896, he was a respected lawyer and
journalist with a reputation for eloquence and hard
work. At the time of his appointment, he was serving
as vice-president of the chamber.

In addition to a solid general record, Varenne
also possessed specific talents and attitudes which
made him an attractive candidate for the highest
colonial position in Indochina. His liberal views
and experience with the liberal press (he had founded
his own newspaper after gaining experience with major
Parisian publications) might have been expected to
give him some common ground with Vietnamese intellectuals. His work on the budgets of the French railroads and communications services and in the colony
of Algeria gave him a degree of financial expertise,

while his service as Minister of Public Education gave him experience in that aspect of social development.[39] Finally, Varenne had served from 1916 to 1919 on a committee for universal suffrage and was held to be a "specialist in electoral reform,"[40] a subject of great interest in Indochina.

Whatever Varenne's qualifications, the Socialist party, for logical reasons, did not approve of its members' accepting colonial appointments. Varenne's own newspaper, *La Montagne*, attempted to point out that he had been pressed to accept the governorship of Tunisia, had refused, and had also turned down an original offer of the same office in Indochina. Only later was he convinced that, because of the potentially dangerous situation in French Asia, he must do the job for his country.[41] The national congress of the Socialist party was not swayed, however, and on August 15, 1925, it was decided in an unprecedented motion that Varenne be expelled from the party's ranks.[42] New independence from the party did not harm Varenne and perhaps not only gave him additional freedom to express his ideas about the French colonial role, but made him somewhat more acceptable to conservatives and Vietnamese, alike. With great expectancy the moderate Vietnamese nationalist Bùi Quang Chiêu wrote from Paris before interviewing Varenne, "We are going to find ourselves facing a man who represents neither party nor caste nor any interest group, but France, the clear French spirit of good sense, reason, and solidarity."[43]

In his statements to the press and at various gatherings of well-wishers, Varenne was careful to express a cautious but hopeful attitude toward Indochinese problems. He made it clear that he had not lost his liberal approach, remarking to a Paris reporter that he would not wear the traditional uniform of the governor general, since "when (*the Vietnamese*) admire those beautiful embroideries, they know full well that they are paying for them."[44] But, at the same time, broad policy speeches revealed that, while reforms were needed, they would be carried out within the existing colonial framework. Conservatives might worry over some of Varenne's specific suggestions, but they approved of his phraseology, which rang unmistakably with tones of the *mission civilisatrice*. "It is not," he said, "for vainglory or for the desire to parade herself that (*France*) goes into this far-off exile; it is not to affirm the rule of the strongest over the weakest; it is to affirm the right and duty of the strongest to protect the weakest; to bring to this beautiful colony the breath of life from our democratic civilization."[45]

French commentators in the Paris press survived

the initial shock of Varenne's appointment and were
nearly unanimous in expressing their confidence that
the decision had been a wise one.[46] Vietnamese
residing in France greeted the news with warm praise
and high hopes. Their remarks are somewhat surprising in the light of Varenne's explicit warning to
them in interviews that it was "better to be deceived
today by my reserve than tomorrow by my acts."[47]
Dương Văn Giao, a Saigon lawyer and one of three
founders of the Constitutionalist party, wrote from
France: "The government of the Republic seems at
last to have agreed to send a little light among the
shadows which have accumulated in Indochina over the
years. . . . We receive the nomination with satisfaction."[48] Bùi Quang Chiêu, another founder of the
Constitutionalist party, sent word to Saigon that he
had the impression that Varenne understood the Indochinese situation in depth. "Paris is forging the
future," he added. "We are finished with regimes of
exploitation and spoliation! Finished with grotesque
policies and puerile assimilation! The people
speak!"[49]

Bùi Quang Chiêu's champagne review reached
Saigon several days before Varenne's arrival there on
November 18, 1925. It undoubtedly was responsible
for heightening the expectations of Vietnamese intellectuals and the small group of Frenchmen who sought

reform. André Malraux, then living in Saigon, expressed the hopes of both when he said that "the arrival of M. Varenne, of the socialist Varenne, ought not only to mark the end of the period of Administration crimes but also to toll the inescapable, necessary hour of retribution."[50]

The administration and business interests, by contrast, had early recorded their discomfort at Varenne's appointment. Government-supported newspapers called the new governor general a "militant socialist" and said that he would "have to serve an apprenticeship."[51] Colonials were particularly concerned when it was reported that the Minister of Colonies, Andre Hessé, and even Painlevé, himself, felt there was no danger of bolshevism in Indochina and supported fully the plans which Varenne had in mind.[52] The news came as an unpleasant revelation to government workers and capitalists in Indochina, and these men not only continued their pressure on Vietnamese intellectuals, but took up a vicious campaign against Varenne and the type of control from home which he represented.

The new issue of the Socialist governor became basic to the building of tension in Indochina in 1925, but old disagreements and fears were rekindled by events which occurred before Varenne's arrival in Saigon. On June 26, 1925, the Vietnamese patriot

Phan Châu Trinh returned to his homeland and made a
number of anticolonial remarks, which received wide
currency. A mere four days afterwards, Phan Bội
Châu, a long-time nationalist agitator, was arrested
in the French concession in Shanghai and returned to
Annam for sentencing. The two instances served to
excite anti-Vietnamese feeling among colonials and
to support Vietnamese fears of the repressive
administration.

On November 6, 1925, Emperor Khải Định died in
Huế, and colonial authorities took the occasion to
reserve for their government most of the remaining
imperial powers.[53] The act was not wholly unprogres-
sive or unpopular. Many Vietnamese reformers would
have preferred to do away with the emperor altogether,
especially since they thought little of imperial
justice.[54] But colonial opinion was, for the most
part, hostile, especially after one French official
stated that the change which had taken place was
"the first step . . . toward the organization of a
constitutional monarchy in which the king reigns but
does not rule."[55] To the stability-conscious, pro-
tectionist colonial, such a suggestion was a threat
to the entire colonial structure.

As if these controversies were not enough,
Cochinchina in 1925 was the scene of numerous serious
scandals involving the colonial administration.

Utilized as ammunition by Saigon liberals, information on the illegal dealings of important officials
filled the opposition press. The government-backed
newspapers returned with counterallegations, and
Governor Cognacq, who was deeply implicated by the
exposés, personally attempted to have the liberal
papers shut down.[56]

The quarrel was not a pretty one, and after the
news about Varenne appeared in the Saigon papers on
July 30, 1925, it became vicious and cruel. André
Malraux, who had found local financial and moral
backing for his magazine-newspapers *L'Indochine* and,
later, *L'Indochine Enchaînée,* described Cognacq in
print as a "disgusting baboon"[57] and "a bugger . . .
in the fullest meaning of the word."[58] The governor
tried desperately to close Malraux's operation by
physical force and through an "anti-Bolshevik" campaign, but was unsuccessful. Threats and counter-
threats grew so violent by November that it seemed
certain that Varenne would act immediately to put
things straight once he set foot on Indochinese soil

Although he could not have been aware of the
intricacy of issues disturbing government and intellectual circles on his arrival, Alexandre Varenne wa
a good politician and sought to remain popular but
uncommitted to any specific course of action. In an
impromptu speech before the crowd that greeted him

in Saigon on November 18, 1925, he said that, while
his administration would be scrupulous, hard-working,
and just, he was not going to make any wild promises
or issue any manifestos.[59] For these sentiments he
was politely applauded, but Vietnamese began to be
concerned that Varenne might be shielded from the
truth and therefore be inclined to take no action at
all. The government made such elaborate plans for
Varenne's official reception that Vietnamese, except
for those under the governor's thumb, found it impossible to approach him.[60] Accordingly, Malraux published an open letter to Varenne, emphasizing irregu-
larities in the Cochinchina administration and
hoping for their correction. On November 24, Vietnamese members of the Colonial Council refused to
approve the budget and denounced Governor Cognacq's
Green Book report on the condition of the colony,
which they felt misrepresented the true state of
affairs.[61] The next day, *La Cloche Fêlée*, a newspaper run by the nationalist-reformer Nguyễn An Ninh,
reappeared, after a period of having been suppressed,
with the subtitle "Organ of Democratic Propaganda"
under its masthead.[62] It hoped to inform the new
governor general of the aspirations of Vietnamese
reformers.

By far the most effective and disciplined effort
to bend Varenne's ear, however, was organized by

Nguyễn Phan Long. This moderate reformer, using his
liberal but usually cautious newspaper *L'Echo Annamite,* encouraged sympathetic Vietnamese to help him
present Varenne with a polished statement of their
grievances. Realizing that the administration in
Saigon might prevent his group from meeting Varenne
before he moved on to the government seat in Hanoi,
Long cabled the governor general's ship in Colombo
on November 7 to request an audience. Varenne agreed
and set the date for November 27.

When the time arrived, Nguyễn Phan Long and
seven hundred followers greeted Varenne in a peaceful
and orderly fashion. After a long address expressing
his loyalty to France and his desire to arrive at a
just solution, Long turned over to Varenne an eloquent written statement known as the *Cahier des Voeux
Annamites.*[63] The *Cahier*, later reprinted in pamphlet
form, became the platform of the Vietnamese moderate
reformist movement.[64] It requested for indigenes
freedom of assembly, association, press, and movement; more representation on local assemblies; and
greater access to government jobs. It was by no
means a revolutionary tract, but in clear terms it
presented propositions and reasons for making
important changes.

There is some dispute as to the full content
and implication of Varenne's return speech at the

meeting, since the two available accounts are found in newspapers of strongly differing bias. But it is probable that there were no radical departures toward either liberal or conservative viewpoints. Varenne said that he had been advised of Vietnamese views in Paris and, while he treated his ideas on reform provisionally, he was certain that his job in Indochina was to undertake reforms of some kind.[65] He nevertheless warned the Vietnamese against hasty and rash acts, expressed reserve about the issue of freedom of the press, and did not touch on the problem of citizenship and higher education.[66] "I beg of you," he concluded, "do not be blindly confident in me, but give me a chance to bring my projects to maturity."[67]

Under normal circumstances, caution of this sort might have been acceptable, and, indeed, there were a few cries of "Vive Varenne!" with applause at appropriate points in the speech. But Varenne at one juncture noted that he intended to make no change regarding personal liberties in Cochinchina, in particular, or in Indochina as a whole,[68] and this stand was a rude disappointment to the moderate Vietnamese reformers, who had worked so hard to gain recognition. Nguyễn Phan Long expressed his discouragement when he warned his countrymen against approaching Varenne "carried on the rapid but fragile

wings of hope" and said, "We have the impression that
once again the Vietnamese will have a chance to
verify the words of (*ex-Governor General*) Maurice
Long: 'Governmental ideas are too often betrayed
by administrative acts.'"[69] Others were not so mild.
Malraux wrote with disgust, "Yesterday a Socialist,
today an outstanding conservative among prominent
conservatives; another conversion under the sign of
the piaster."[70] *La Cloche Fêlée* echoed with, "To
believe that our present governor general will remain
a militant socialist is to believe in the sincerity
of the devil or of a wolf in sheep's clothing. From
a militant Socialist, M. Varenne has been transformed
into a colonialist, plain and simple."[71]

How much the poor reception from the Vietnamese
press influenced Varenne is uncertain, but he cannot
have been pleased at having alienated both the Vietnamese and the colonials. In a speech before the
Council of Government in Hanoi on December 20, 1925,
Varenne made a concerted effort to specify the programs he was considering, but to do so in such a way
as to restore all groups' confidence in him. Appealing to Vietnamese sentiments, he offered the opinion:

> Indochina has become conscious of herself,
> she looks to the future and searches for her
> destiny. What will her future be? If peace
> is kept, if the people of Indochina can
> develop freely . . . she can hope to attain

one day the fullest and highest of exist-
ences, that of a nation.

France can aid her. She will aid her.
She will fulfill to the very end the mandate
which is traditionally hers, which is to
illuminate and gather around her individuals
and peoples.

Her mission achieved, one could think
that she will have left in Indochina only
a souvenir of her work, that she will claim
no role in the life of the peninsula, neither in directing or even counseling, and
that the peoples who will have benefited
from her tutelage will have no ties with
her except those of gratitude and affection.[72]

To soothe administrative and colonial nerves, he

affirmed:

I do not bring with me a new doctrine; I
come simply to affirm the meaning of our
colonizing mission with its highly civilized, humanitarian, disinterested character . . . [we must maintain] a spirit
of order, method, and sincerity. . . .[73]

It was an impressive effort, but an unsuccessful one.

The Vietnamese press hardly mentioned the speech and

certainly remained unexcited by the references to

freedom, though they were the first ever made in a

speech by a governor general of Indochina. Nguyễn

Phan Long limited his comment to the terse admission

that he was reassured of Varenne's intentions but

"waited impatiently for action."[74]

The reaction of the colonials was not made clear

until several months later. In March 1926 the Chamber of Deputies in Paris was thrown into an uproar when it was reported that its representative in Indochina had promised independence to the Vietnamese. People clamored for Varenne's removal, and the Paris press commented unfavorably on the affair.[75] The outcry, however, died down as quickly as it had sprung up. Varenne publicly explained that the controversial portion of his speech had been lifted out of context and presented to certain people by his political enemies in the Indochinese administration in order to achieve his recall.[76] He kept his job, but that experience and others like it made him distrustful of the Indochinese press, whether in French or Vietnamese hands, and also increased his distaste for the entanglements of local politics.

If Varenne was annoyed to find himself caught in the cross fire of personal local antagonisms, he can only have been dismayed when political issues of far broader significance were laid at his feet. The first of these concerned Phan Bội Châu. As mentioned earlier, the nationalist had been arrested in Shanghai and returned to Annam in July 1925. Varenne, aware of the potential ill effects of sentencing a popular figure like Châu to death or imprisonment, had hoped to avoid the entire affair. To a reporter

117

who questioned him in Paris on the subject he replied, "What do you see in that business that might harm me? It is all strange to me; the Phan Bội Châu trial will certainly be finished, in two months, when I arrive in Indochina. There are laws there which should take care of things like this quickly."[77]

Châu's trial, however, was not concluded until Varenne had been in Indochina for several days. On November 23, 1925, he was sentenced to forced labor for life, and French and Vietnamese liberals voiced their disapproval. Châu's past had been one of continued and usually radical opposition to the French,[78] and in 1925 he had been with Hồ Chí Minh in Canton, founding the Association of Revolutionary Vietnamese Youth. Such a background did not appear savory to many in Indochina, but the circumstances of Châu's arrest led even some conservative Frenchmen to express their concern. It was probably not widely known that the Sûreté had paid 100,000 piasters to have Phan Bội Châu delivered into their hands,[79] but the general feeling was that the excuses given for the arrest were weak and the methods unknown, and therefore suspect. The normally restrained and pro-government paper *Argus Indochinoise* editorialized to Varenne when he arrived in Hanoi on December 5, 1925: "Not to accord full and complete amnesty to

Phan Bội Châu would be the gravest of political er-
rors because it would cause the indigene to doubt
your fundamental magnanimity and the sincerity of
your affection for him."[80] Expressing their own
sentiments in a more radical fashion, students in
Hanoi greeted Varenne with cries of "Phan Bội Châu
free, or trouble!"[81]

It was not easy to assess public opinion
completely or accurately, and Varenne had difficulty
in arriving at a decision. On the one hand, he was
sent numerous pleas to pardon Châu, and, on the
other, members of the Sûreté and the Tongking
administration tried to impress him with the dangers
of bolshevism,[82] while tracts were circulated showing the prisoner to be more radical than he may
perhaps in fact have been.[83] Varenne's response
was to leave the sentence as it had been handed down
until he could check with Paris.[84]

The Ministry of Colonies refused to act for
Varenne. Various colonial experts, including Sarraut,
conferred and concluded that Varenne was better
placed than they to make the decision.[85] Varenne
pardoned Phan Bội Châu on December 23, 1925, and
permitted him to return to Annam under the condition
that he not leave his village without the permission
of the Sûreté.[86] This compromise action was more
successful than earlier attempts at verbal com-

promise, and Varenne received the thanks of students
and intellectuals, many of whom he had previously
alienated. Administrators and colonials did not,
for the most part, exhibit their disappointment, perhaps because Paris was clearly supporting Varenne
and because Châu would be kept under the control of
the government.

Phan Bội Châu, however, needed only to be
present in Indochina to inspire continued nationalist
pressure on the government. He was careful to adopt
a pro-French attitude and to remain unembroiled in
local affairs, but his experience became widely discussed. When it was learned that he was in desperate
need of money, collections were taken up by Vietnamese newspapers and other organizations; and the
effort kept Châu in the public eye. Vietnamese
intellectuals who had earlier been attracted by the
possibilities of convincing Varenne to make important
political changes in Indochina saw in this period of
heightened public interest and seeming willingness by
the governor general to listen to public opinion, the
perfect moment to step up their reform campaign. It
was to be a loyalist, moderate drive, but one which
sought to impress the French with its determination;
it would be ready to accept all manner of compromise,
but it must be recognized and given a clear, direct
reply.

Of the Vietnamese leaders active during the
crucial early months of 1926, the most powerful and
respected was probably Bùi Quang Chiêu. A naturalized French citizen, he had great hopes for his
native land and the highest respect for France. The
core of his political thought was cooperation between
the two for the enrichment of both. In 1917, as a
government official and agricultural engineer, Bùi
Quang Chiêu founded *La Tribune Indigène*, a newspaper
supporting the progressive policies of the current
governor general, Albert Sarraut.[87] Five years
later, with two other men, he established the Constitutionalist party, Indochina's first legal political
organization. It was tolerated largely because "it
managed to establish some connections with liberal
forces in metropolitan France,"[88] but it was closely
surveyed by the Sûreté and subjected to restrictions.

The platform of the Constitutionalist party,
as Chiêu conceived it, could not be constructed of
specific demands or intricate theoretical assump-
tions. It would have to gain its strength from both
French and Vietnamese groups, and in order to do so,
a broad, flexible, but appealing concept would have
to be used. Accordingly, the program came to be
stated simply in the slogan "With France, by the
Vietnamese, toward Dominion."[89] With this firmly in
mind, and with the belief that "the bastion of French

influence in the Pacific ought to be Indochina,"[90] Bùi Quang Chiêu spent much of his time touring France giving lectures to large and generally approving crowds. He made it clear that he wished to save Indochina from radicals seeking to force the French out completely[91] and said that the only way to avoid this was to modernize Indochina[92] and thereby inspire a loyalist movement among the Vietnamese people. If popular support for the French could not be mustered, he warned prophetically:

> In fifteen or twenty years, Indochina will escape French influence, for between France and Indochina exploiters will have raised a wall of hate. Our people will then be at the mercy of the first aggressor who comes along or the first savior to present himself. . . .[93]

Bùi Quang Chiêu spent much effort in France attempting to garner public and official support there for his ideas. In Saigon, fellow Constitutionalist Nguyễn Phan Long voiced similar opinions and worked hard to protect Vietnamese interests. Scrupulously moderate in tone on most occasions, he wrote for, and after mid-1922 published, *L'Echo Annamite*, a newspaper directed at Vietnamese functionaries and intellectuals. The original goal of *L'Echo*, when it was founded in 1920 by Võ Văn Thơm, was to "serve the superior interest of France and

Indochina" and to guide the rational, peaceful
development of the Vietnamese people;[94] and Long
later subscribed to the same line, noting that he
wished to avoid violence and hatred, but to achieve
justice in mild temper.[95] His main quarrel with the
administration seems to have **concerned** corruption
and the barring of Vietnamese from economic affairs
and higher government posts.

Nguyễn Phan Long, unlike Bùi Quang Chiêu, was
not a French citizen and tended to be more deeply
involved with specifically Vietnamese aspirations
and the question of racism. After experiencing
frustration in making himself heard in administrative
circles, Long apparently became convinced that the
Vietnamese would have to take greater pride in themselves and unite to speak in one voice if they expected anyone to listen. In January 1924 *L'Echo
Annamite* began publishing again after six months of
idleness and, in all probability, government pressure.[96] Long took the occasion to restate his aims
and revealed the new direction of his thinking:

> The ideal of our newspaper, written by com-
> patriots for compatriots, is the general
> well-being of the Vietnamese people. And
> its source is a profound love . . . for
> this land of Vietnam, to which we are at-
> tached by all the fibers of our being and
> in which we will sleep our last sleep.
> . . . .
> We invite the Vietnamese public to collab-

orate with us to make this paper their paper,
to work together to have a little more good
will and well-being among the masses of
Vietnam, to make Cochinchina richer, more
prosperous, and in reality a France of the
Far East, in the fullest meaning of the
term.[97]

While these words did not represent a radical departure from *L'Echo*'s basic policy, they made abun-
dantly clear the newspaper's dissatisfaction with
the assimilationist policy as it had been carried
out in the past, contained more than a suggestion of
strong nationalist sentiment, and sought to plant
the seeds of a mass movement.

Nguyễn Phan Long left the confines of controlled
criticism of the local scene and passed into the
broad political field. He was aware of the dangers
involved, but risked them because there seemed no
other way to acquire an audience that would take
him seriously. One of his best editorials, printed
shortly after the reopening of *L'Echo* in 1924, expressed his bitterness at the refusal of the French
administrators and colonials to listen, their
determination to silence all true political activity,
and the timidity of the Vietnamese who had found
jobs in the administration:

They scream at us: "No politics!" . . . .
What they mean is: Don't make any politics
different from those of the government.

. . . .
The word *politics* takes on a sense of mys-
tery, of horror, the more so since it is
vague and ill-defined. Applied to those
who do not think as the government does,
it evokes, in the fertile imaginations of
those who always want to have someone or
something to save, notions of secret meetings, plottings, or at least subversive
opinions, capable of upsetting the indiges-
tions of the Doctor Panglosses who are so
optimistic in normal times that they are
prompted to lose their heads at the
slightest difficulty.
. . . .
The loyalists all shout at full pitch from
the rooftops, "I'm not involved in any
politics!" as if they were denying having
murdered their parents! And they end up
receiving the profitable approval of the
government.
. . . .
I am an official, you say. But does being
invested with a public function make one
cease being a man, a citizen participating
in the fortune of his country?
. . . .
What people call politics [is nothing more
than] the act of a citizen, or simply a man,
an honest man . . . .
. . . .
The Republic would not exist in France today, perhaps, if courageous men, treated
like criminals or lunatics, had not, in
dreaming of liberty, worked passionately
for its achievement.[98]

Long not only wrote in defense of his ideas, but
he acted to make them effective and to spread them to
others. In a careful campaign he won a seat on the
Colonial Council of Cochinchina. As already mentioned, he took Vietnamese grievances directly to
Varenne and, though disappointed at the initial response, continued his efforts in his newspaper. He

even joined the Young Annam movement, supposedly
founded by André Malraux in 1925.[99]   But even this
suspiciously activist group, perhaps under Long's
influence, had for its goal in Cochinchina the
"vindication, *by all legal means,* of the people's
legitimate right, particularly human and civil
rights" (italics in the original).[100]   A firm moderate who found it difficult but necessary to walk the
line between inaction and revolution, Nguyễn Phan
Long had a view of the future that was hopeful and
steady:

> The future is ours; time works for us.   In
> ten years, twenty, or more, the new law of
> humanity will be affirmed and the situa-
> tion . . . will be changed to the degree
> that what today is regarded as a mark of
> liberalism will appear as something natu-
> rally due.[101]

A third would-be reformer, Nguyễn An Ninh, published in Saigon *La Cloche Fêlée,* a newspaper echoing
moderate ideas in a more literary and often more
insistent tone than organs like *L'Echo Annamite.*
Ninh had close ties with Malraux and his associate
Paul Monin, a long-time resident of Indochina with a
reputation for being a militant and fearless liberal,
and may have been influenced by the style and approach expressed by these two Frenchmen in their
often vitriolic magazine, *L'Indochine.*   He also

became friendly with Léon Werth, a Socialist writer who visited Indochina and contributed articles of protest to the various liberal publications there. Werth became intrigued by Ninh, finding him the perfect example of an intellectual caught between the two worlds of Vietnam and France, a lesson in the follies of assimilation. On the one hand, Ninh was devoted to bettering the lot and consciousness of the Vietnamese masses and spoke of the necessity for youth "above all to speak of nation and patriotism" if it would lead the country,[102] while, on the other, he sometimes acted more European than Werth, himself,[103] and had great faith in France and French institutions. He called upon his countrymen to "unmask all those who call themselves French (or supporters of the French) but who work against France, who prepare a generation hostile to France. France has given you rights; show that you know how to guard them, and She will give you more."[104]

In general, Nguyễn An Ninh did not find it intolerable for France to administer Indochina, but he had serious misgivings about the way she was doing it in the 1920s.[105] He thought that a rebellion against the corruption of race-hatred which he saw in French colonialism would be justified, but preferred conciliation and compromise. In the long run, he hoped, "a time will come when we can better enjoy

127

living in this country . . . . France will see her
own children and her adopted ones united in one tradition to make Indochina a France in Asia."[106]

But Ninh was embittered and frustrated by the
difficulty of realizing the kind of future he
envisioned, and he expressed his feelings with a
sensitive and energetic pen. He admonished Vietnamese youth that their real struggle was against
their environment--the families and society which
made them narrow, uninspired, and inactive--and
warned them to pay no attention to the administration's plea for quiet and order:

> They speak to us about ingratitude, immor-
> ality, anarchy, but don't listen to these
> reactionaries, our poisoners . . . . They
> speak about anarchy--but what do they call
> anarchy? What do they call order? What is
> their "order" if it isn't coercion, bar-
> barousness, anarchy?[107]

It was not long before such rhetorical questioning,
coupled with increasing disappointment over unful-
filled French promises, disillusionment with Varenne,
and a continued inability to bring about any significant change in the colonial administration, led
Ninh to pronounce some sweeping condemnations of not
only the Indochinese situation, but French colonialism as a whole. Though he was still pro-French when
he wrote it, the following passage illustrates very

well the angry and resentful position Ninh began to take:

> People often speak of the educative, civi-
> lizing role of France, represented by the
> group now in control. They have paid homage
> to the "bringers of light," to the "makers
> of miracles in Asia," as if the boors sent
> out by the Ministry of Colonies rather than
> intellectual France could, with some sort
> of dough, fashion in a short time the soul
> of a race whose every work was perfect.
> People speak of the French miracles in Asia,
> and they even have a book by that name.
> What is the miracle? It is a miracle, real-
> ly, that power can, in a short time, lower
> to the point of thick ignorance an intel-
> lectual level which was already low enough.
> It is a miracle that power can, in such a
> short time, lead people to democratic
> ideas while they are in complete servitude.
> Who would say that it isn't a miracle, a
> social miracle, the sudden realization of
> a state which people need thousands of
> years to reach *(under normal circumstances)*?
> Are not ignorance and inaction the two
> primary conditions for happiness? To speak
> of the educative, civilizing role of the
> masters of Indochina, gentlemen, that makes
> me laugh. Those who officially represent
> France in Indochina can only talk of
> expensive construction, railroads, ruinous
> attempts to lay submarine cables, of the
> maintenance of a formidable army of func-
> tionaries, of the annual national loans, in
> short, of the excessive exploitation of
> Indochina, of exploitation in two senses of
> the word. It is, above all, economic, that
> is to say, devouring. But when it is a
> question of more delicate matters, of educa-
> tion and intellectual growth, France appears
> to be hesitant. She can only bring us her
> intellectual heritage *(insofar as it helps)*
> to feed explorers and inventors. Assimila-
> tion requires freedom of choice, absolute
> freedom. All coercion leads to indigestion,
> and indigestion can be fatal.[108]

129

Tongking's most important Vietnamese reformer,
Phạm Quỳnh, was an influential mandarin and teacher-
scholar who began publicizing his ideas around 1917.
He is usually described as a monarchist and therefore somewhat apart from other reformers, but he
expressed his feeling on numerous occasions that
Indochina would need a constitution as well as a
monarch if it wished to modernize. Quỳnh did differ,
however, from most activists of his day in his
emphasis on the traditional Vietnamese elite, of
whose mandarinate he was a member, and its ability
to provide the necessary inspiration and leadership
to take the country into a modern, just, and humanitarian age. To men like Nguyễn Phan Long and Nguyễn
An Ninh, such thinking was automatically suspect,
since it sought to preserve what they considered to
be a decaying institution, full of its own faults
and further corrupted by the French. But Phạm
Quỳnh's scheme, it is often forgotten, did call for
some thoroughgoing changes in the mandarinate. He
admitted that many individuals set bad examples, but
held that on the whole it was a good and useful
institution which needed only careful treatment and
the proper personnel to perform creditably.[109] The
traditional elite, he said, possessed elements
capable of modernizing Vietnam:

It (*was only*) a question of getting them
together and giving them a common inspiration. The sole idea capable of doing this--
of creating this union, or spiritual unity--
is, incontestably, the national idea. One
cannot deny that this idea exists in the
country; the fact is that it grows, develops, intensifies every day. Nothing will
be served by hemming it in, stopping it; it
is better to utilize it, channel it, and
make it the basis of the education of the
masses as well as of the elite. Then we
will see that it is a great force, capable
of solving everything if each of us knows
how to do his part.[110]

With a refurbished and reoriented elite, Phạm
Quỳnh thought that a compromise between Vietnamese
nationalism and the Indochinese Union could be
reached within the framework of the protectorate.
By 1980, he expected, Vietnam would be a "great
nation," a "free state in the structure of the French
Empire."[111] For the present, French rule was a
fact, but if it were accepted calmly and if extrem-
ism were avoided, the situation would gradually
improve.[112]

For all his moderation, patience, and loyalty
to France, Phạm Quỳnh was outspoken in his defense
of the right of Vietnamese to speak and act on
political issues. While he did not approve of de-
structive politics, he warned the French that to ask
Vietnamese to avoid the kind of politics that was
undertaken for the general good was to ask that they
"be disinterested in the fate of their country, in

131

the future of their children, in the well-being of
their families, and even in their own lives."[113] To
French colonials who spoke hopefully of the Vietnamese one day becoming Eurasians, thinking and acting as much like Europeans as Asians and having no
basis for nationalist feeling, he replied that such
ideas were too futuristic:

> We will perhaps be, one day, "Eurasians."
> In the meantime, we are, and will be for a
> long time yet, Vietnamese. We hope to live
> a full national life, and we ask that France
> help us do so. There lies the entire ques-
> tion.[116]

Despite the difficulties he saw in arriving at a
solution, Phạm Quỳnh remained convinced that Franco-
Vietnamese collaboration not only would be a success,
but was in truth the best possible combination. He
wrote, in one of his more fanciful moments, that the
French and Vietnamese could not, for example, be
compared with the British and Indian peoples; the
latter pair was an unpleasant blend of merchants and
mystics, while the former consisted of peoples who
were both "profoundly human."[117] The British were
imperialists, while the French were not, since being
French was a "state of mind."[118]

The majority of French colonials found it impossible to accept the ideas of the moderate Vietnamese

intellectuals. In many instances colonials simply did not understand much of the argumentation used by those who urged reform, and regarded their abstractions, their talk of French heritage and traditional liberalism, as verbal camouflage for bolshevism, and nothing more. The attitude is nowhere better illustrated than in the famous incident when Nguyễn An Ninh was brought before Governor Cognacq to explain certain of his opinions which had appeared in *La Cloche Fêlée*. Ninh talked about the necessity of freedom of the press and free exchange of ideas to a successful meeting of the French and Vietnamese worlds, but Cognacq cut him off: "In this country, we don't need any intellectuals! The country is too simple. If you want to intellectualize, go to Moscow."[119] Cognacq was, perhaps, an extreme example of a man who cried "Bolshevik" at the slightest provocation, and even members of the administration thought him rather radical in that regard, but the tendency was widespread to apply the term *anti-French* to all those, French or Vietnamese, who questioned the administration.[120]

More thoughtful colonial opinion accepted the existence of Vietnamese intellectuals--though not always their ideas--on special terms and in a special position. According to this point of view:

133

> (*Well-educated Vietnamese*) could accomplish
> a very wonderful task; in living independ-
> ently, away from even the watchfulness of
> the government, they could be veritable
> mouthpieces of the indigenous population,
> could be preserving but moderate interpret-
> ers of the certain aspirations and certain
> legitimate desires of an agricultural peo-
> ple, instead of becoming for their com-
> patriots the hateful dictators of discon-
> tent.[121]

The kind of assimilation which made a limited elite
into the middlemen between French colonials and the
Vietnamese people was not what any of the Vietnamese
reformers wanted. The most moderate of them, Phạm
Quỳnh, once defined assimilation as "nothing less
than the transforming of the mentality of an entire
people by their acquisition of qualities which they
have heretofore lacked,"[122] and this was quite different from what the colonials, and perhaps even
Paris, intended by assimilation or, for that matter,
by association.

Colonials found it impossible even to consider
that France had given the Vietnamese intellectual
ammunition to use against the absolutist colonial
regime. Or, if the fact was recognized, it was not
condoned. Not legally permitted in either Cochinchina or any of the protectorates, the works of
Montesquieu, Rousseau, and others were nevertheless
secretly passed about in elite circles and read with
great interest.[123] Phạm Quỳnh was fond of saying

that "today's malcontents are malcontents in the
French manner, for French reasons,"[124] while Nguyễn
An Ninh put it more simply in the maxim that "oppression comes to us from France, but so does the spirit
of liberation."[125] Because it found itself under
attack, the colonial government permitted itself to
label as anti-French the very people who were best-
versed in French studies, who most fully supported
French ideas, and who were best trained and suited
not to hate France and her empire. The attitude
not only created tension and encouraged the petty
hatred of those who did not feel intellectually
attached to France, but blocked progress and did
little to shore up or supplement Vietnamese tradition, as it slowly declined under French influence.
The situation, as the moderate Dường Văn Giao
assessed it, was critical and admitted of two possible solutions, one of which was attractive but not
within reach, the other of which was becoming more
and more likely:

> The colonials, the administrators--
> governors included--are men that come and
> go. The country, alas, remains--the peo-
> ple remain; the tradition, however . . .
> goes on, carried on ignorance, and evolu-
> tion does not take place. If this state
> of things continues, revolution will come
> along. When evolution is not possible,
> revolution is.[126]

In the spring of 1926 it seemed to many Frenchmen that revolution had indeed come to Indochina.
In Saigon on the morning of March 21, a demonstration, probably organized by the Young Annam group, of
which Nguyễn Phan Long and Nguyễn An Ninh were
listed as secretaries, protested the expulsion policy
of the Cochinchina government and reiterated the
demands made in the *Cahier des Voeux Annamites* for
the freedoms of press and assembly. The crowd ended
the outdoor meeting with cries of "Vive Vietnam!"[127]
It was probably at this time that inflammatory
tracts began to appear in the streets:

> Brothers! We have been slaves for seventy
> years. During that time a tyrannical
> government has oppressed us. Today it asks
> us to love *(it)* and actually pretends to
> carry us toward a better civilization. It
> preaches an entente between the conqueror
> and the conquered . . . . If we do not con-
> sider our own destiny, no one else
> will . . . . But we are impotent and un-
> able to accomplish anything against the
> government. However, we can unite and
> show that we have a despotic ruler over
> us . . . . Here we stand on the soil of
> our ancestors. We should march from north
> to south. If the government asks the local
> officials where they can expel us, we re-
> ply--To Moscow . . . . The people of [Viet-
> nam] should take up arms and drive the
> invaders from our land. Why do we hesi-
> tate? Under the pretext of accomplishing
> a civilizing mission, France has reduced
> us to slavery. We are treated like buffalo
> and horses. Let us unite, because numbers
> make strength and we are millions against a
> few thousand French.[128]

The authorship of this radical propaganda is uncertain, and its relationship to men like Nguyễn Phan Long is unknown. But two weeks later Nguyễn An Ninh's *La Cloche Fêlée* began to print the Communist Manifesto in serial form,[129] and it became clear that the nature of the reform movement was becoming confused. Worse, the apparent change in ideology of some reformers confirmed the greatest fears of the French colonials.

On March 24, 1926, coincidence had it that two events of great importance to Vietnamese nationalists and reformers took place. The first of these was the arrival in Saigon of Bùi Quang Chiêu, an occasion which had been advertised in *L'Echo Annamite* for two weeks before. When Chiêu disembarked, he found that the two groups who had come to meet him--several thousand Vietnamese and several hundred Frenchmen-- were threatening to come to blows and begin a riot of no mean proportion. The details of the incident are unimportant, but it appears that the colonials' demonstration, in which Chiêu was booed and hissed, was deliberately organized to goad the Vietnamese assembly, which was under Nguyễn Phan Long's leadership, into violent reaction. If it had been successful, it would have been possible for the administration to silence the reformist groups and newspapers by force, under the pretense that they were violent revolutionaries, Bolsheviks, Communists, and anarchists.[130] To the credit of the Vietnamese, they remained peaceful and did not resist when police took control and sent the rallies home. The news of the demonstration was quickly spread, with great emphasis being placed upon the thwarted plans of the colonials, and it became the object of heated discussion.

One of the results of the Bùi Quang Chiêu affair was that the underhanded dealings of a close group of reactionaries in Cochinchina were made clear. These men were the same who had carried on the campaign against Varenne since his arrival, and they had, in fact, seen their demonstration as a method of embarrassing the governor general and thwarting his plans.[131] It is not evident exactly how he has able to do so, but Varenne finally seized upon the implications of the colonials' reactionary attitude and actions and had Cognacq removed[132] and the more obvious of his associates exposed and silenced, or at least made uncomfortable. For the time being, Varenne was free of the vindictive backbiting he had earlier experienced from the colonials.

At the same time, however, Varenne was not slow to realize that the show of Vietnamese support for Bùi Quang Chiêu and the exhibit of discipline were intended to impress the government with the necessity of reform. No one was certain to what degree it was so, but the insistence with which even the mildest of reformers began to speak indicated that the entire movement might be taking a radical turn. It also appeared capable of gathering broader support than many Frenchmen had suspected.

The second important event of March 24, 1926, the death of the nationalist Phan Châu Trinh,[133] had long-range effects which seemed to confirm Varenne's worst fears. Trinh was a mandarin who was a harsh critic of both his own people and the French; he supported the French protectorate, but in 1906 had memorialized Governor General Beau about the misery of the people and the corruption of the mandarinal system.[134] Trinh had originally been associated with Phan Bội Châu and had traveled with him to Japan, where young Vietnamese patriots were gathering, but had become suspicious of Châu's revolutionary intentions and returned home. There he founded the Tongking Free School and concentrated his efforts on elevating the Vietnamese through popular education. In 1908 Trinh was arrested because of the involvement of some of his students in the disturbances of that year. He was deported to Poulo Condore with other political prisoners, freed three years later, and allowed to retire to France, where he became connected with various leftist groups. He

was associated for a time with Hồ Chí Minh in Paris.
On July 26, 1925, Trinh returned to Vietnam but did
not, from external evidence at least, become directly involved in any of the controversies going on at
that time.

It is extraordinarily difficult to characterize
Phan Châu Trinh and his thought in a few words. A
French scholar noted for his fair appraisal of
Vietnamese nationalist sentiments called Trinh a
"revolutionary republican,"[135] while an American
writer devised the somewhat confusing label, "non-
revolutionary reformist-agitator."[136] Certainly
there were elements in Trinh's thinking and circle
of friends that bespoke radicalism, but Trinh, for
the most part, seems to have held that a liberation
by force of arms was undesirable.[137] He respected
France and her institutions and once said, "Grant us
the same law as Frenchmen, and we shall ask nothing
better than to live under the aegis of France!
French law for everyone!"[138] To Vietnamese who,
like himself, asked for reform of the colonial
system Trinh advised:

>Be united as a single man in demanding your
>legitimate rights. Write in the newspa-
>pers, set forth your wants, appeal to the
>humanitarian ideals of France . . . . You
>will receive satisfaction after you ask
>for justice.[139]

On the afternoon of March 24, at a tea honoring
Bùi Quang Chiêu in Saigon, the Sûreté arrested Nguyễn An Ninh, a part-Chinese journalist named Lâm
Hiệp Châu, and the half-French progressive writer
Dejean de la Batie. Ninh and de la Batie, who were
both sharp-tongued and quick-witted, had annoyed the
administration with their damaging and increasingly
ferocious attacks in the press. They were also
closely connected to leading nationalist figures.
Evidently, the police believed that the two had been
involved in extremist plots during the demonstration
earlier in the day, so they were accused of scheming
against the Sûreté and inciting revolt.[140] Lâm Hiệp
Châu was accused of inciting revolt through his
eulogy of Phan Châu Trinh, which, unaccountably, had
been printed the day before in the illegal newspaper
Le Jeune Annam.[141] The article had asked whether
Trinh's death ought to be an occasion of national
mourning:

> What is our duty toward a great patriot, a
> martyr for a cause common to us all? Young
> China, for whom Sun Yat-sen freed *(his
> country)* from Western imperialism, trans-
> formed his death into an event of national
> mourning. And what is going to come of the
> death of our Phan Châu Trinh? Will it be
> an event of national mourning for us? It
> will, without doubt. And I believe that it
> ought to be. What do you think! Readers,
> compatriots.[142]

News of the arrests not only inflamed public opinion against the colonial government, but attracted more attention to Phan Châu Trinh's death. When Trinh was buried on April 4, a crowd of ten to fifteen thousand persons paraded in sympathy.[143] At about the same time, students appeared in Hanoi and Saigon wearing crepe armbands and were greeted with cries of alarm from their teachers and the government.[144] Young Vietnamese had used the occasion of Trinh's funeral to voice their criticism of the educational system, complaining of its poor quality and the limitations placed on entrance, but the administration saw only angry nationalist activity and rebellion. The police moved quickly to prevent further disturbances, and on April 11 Varenne wrote a personal letter to the director of public instruction requesting him to take all necessary steps to forestall a repetition of the outbreaks.[145] The tactless handling of the affair,[146] however, encouraged Vietnamese students and intellectuals to continue strikes sporadically through 1926 and 1927 and to remain insistent in their demands.

With the exception of that letter, available sources give little indication of what effect the nationalist-reformist demonstrations had on Alexandre Varenne. Sometime in March 1926 he addressed the Hảiphòng Chamber of Commerce, an almost exclusively

French group, and expressed the opinion that French domination in Indochina was destined to last forever and that French and Vietnamese interests were becoming more and more intertwined.[147] But on another occasion in the same month Varenne noted to a Vietnamese gathering that Indochina would one day be freed by the French.[148]

It was not until September 19, 1926, that the governor general, in a speech to the Council of Government, clarified his attitude toward the events of the past several months and, in broader scope, his views on the entire French role in Indochina. For perhaps the first time since his appointment, Varenne spoke with little equivocation. Beginning with a few remarks about France's civilizing role in Indochina over the past fifty years and praise for the "incomparable pioneers of French civilization, isolated Europeans in the midst of half-savage peoples,"[149] he said:

> Between this regime and the one which exists in France, where the authorities don't hesitate to prohibit meetings if they think it necessary, I don't see such a great difference. Besides, our rôle is not to encourage agitation.[150]

The laws concerning freedom of assembly and bodily constraint were not going to be changed. The intellectuals and reformers represented:

> a fraction . . . a minority, an unstable
> minority, it is certain. I don't turn up
> my nose at minorities, especially *avant-
> garde* minorities. They play a necessary
> rôle in politics. They oblige the public
> powers to continually ask themselves about
> their duties, and encourage them to put
> useful measures into operation. But they
> have a great tendency to misunderstand
> what is offered them in order to vaunt what
> is refused them.[151]

As for the press, Varenne believed that journalism
could aid the rapid education of the masses, but in
Indochina he had only watched it encourage violence
and act irresponsibly. He had wanted to try out a
regime of tolerance before attempting one of complete
freedom, but the press and the opinions it stirred
up had convinced him that the experiment could not
succeed.[152] But France would retain her position in
Indochina despite difficulties and opposition:

> Nothing will keep France from continuing her
> work in Indochina. Those of our Vietnamese
> friends who, accepting French collaboration,
> assign to a far-off date the day when our
> mission will be completely fulfilled, seem to
> forget that Vietnam is not all of Indochina.[153]

There would always be minorities and interest groups
and territories for the French to protect in Indochina, and she would always do so. There might be

objectors and critics hostile to the French, but

> for us French, it is sufficient to know in
> our hearts that we are fulfilling here a
> grand national obligation and a lofty human
> mission.[154]

Varenne was preaching something quite different from the Socialist gospel, but he appeared to believe that his stand was essentially correct. Perhaps he had been chagrined at the discovery, but politics, he now thought, was only disruptive to colonial life and, no matter who practiced it, had no place in Indochina.

In mid-September 1926 Phạm Quỳnh and his moderate supporters met to consider the founding of an officially recognized society which might propagate their ideas. Dismayed at the recent growth of extremist feeling in Indochina, they arrived at a common statement of purpose more quickly than they had thought possible and sent it and requests for recognition to Varenne. The proposed Vietnam People's Progressivist Union (Việt Nam Tấn Bộ Dân Hội) aimed "to work, according to the policy of Franco-Vietnamese collaboration, for the moral, intellectual, and economic education of the people, so that they might participate with the French government in the development of the country."[155]

Phạm Quỳnh explicitly stated that the union was
not intended to be a political party, since political
parties meant only division and opposition, but hoped
to achieve a unified effort in nonpolitical fields to
save the country.[156] Nevertheless, the government
was not impressed and took no official action on the
request for recognition.[157] Quỳnh's group was bitterly disappointed, and the opinion of most moderate
Vietnamese, who felt strongly that Varenne had betrayed the principles he had expounded a year earlier, was summed up by the writer, who concluded somewhat wearily that, "Franco-Vietnamese collaboration
founded on true equality and justice has not yet
found a satisfactory formula in governmental projects
and, even less, in administrative acts."[158] As a
more indignant and sarcastic observer put it:

> Conclusion:
> French liberalism is always translated into
> words, but never into action.
> They tell us that everything comes in time
> to those who know how to wait. And of
> course the Vietnamese will have the pa-
> tience to wait.[159]

Varenne's attitude toward political activity in
Indochina, symbolized by his refusal to legalize the
Progressivist Union, effectively blocked moderate
action for reform among the Vietnamese. When Varenne
arrived in France in early November 1926 for talks

with metropolitan officials, he remarked that "Indochina *(was)* perfectly calm,"[160] and, strictly speaking, that was true. Political activity, however, had
not vanished. Phạm Quỳnh and Bùi Quang Chiêu had
already come under sharp criticism from their associates, who called for less talk and more action.[161]
After Quỳnh was turned down by the colonial government, his political capital lay mostly in the hands
of the radical and Communist-influenced group with
whom the Progressivists had originally split.[162] Bùi
Quang Chiêu still called for a Franco-Vietnamese
rapprochement,[163] but at the same time he was uncon-
vinced that people really wanted a policy of collaboration,[164] so he gave his support to a proposed boycott of French goods. Nguyễn An Ninh, freed after
serving part of a two-year jail sentence, founded an
underground Communist-front organization called the
Hope of Youth party (Cao Vọng Thanh Đẳng).[165] As
time went by, those who, like Nguyễn Phan Long,
refused to use revolutionary methods to achieve their
ends, got nothing for their efforts and began to lose
their combativeness.[166] The reformers who preferred
evolutionary development and partnership depended, in
the last analysis, on French acceptance of their
plans for their success. When that acceptance was
not forthcoming, the movement's policies and persua-
sions were undercut, and it became politically bank-

rupt. Radical underground groups could not help being strengthened and encouraged by the monopoly on political activity with which they were left.

It would be rash to conclude that Alexandre Varenne's stand against the moderate Vietnamese reformers was responsible for Communist control of the nationalist movement or, by extension, for France's loss of Indochina after World War II. Too many developments took place within and outside of Indochina between 1925 and 1954 to make the connection a direct one. It is nevertheless clear that in denying moderate politics the right to exist and to be effective Varenne permitted the political emptiness of the colonial regime to remain legally unfilled. In an era and environment of politicization, the policy was unwise, and the government made enemies of those who might have become friends, or at least collaborators. The official notion, as stated by Varenne, that "the essential condition for progress is the maintenance of emotional calm and respect for public order"[167] only served to tie the colonial government to the unsatisfactory status quo and, in the long run, therefore to increase misunderstanding and tension between French and Vietnamese. Despite, or perhaps even partially because of, the real advances made by Varenne through his social and economic reforms in 1927 and 1928, political pressures on the colonial regime grew, rather than diminished. The more the increasingly radical opposition was forced to hide from public view, the more it inspired French administrators and colonials with an ignorant fear, making them doubly determined to oppose change in Indochina and encouraging them to remain unsympathetic to even the responsible and moderate Vietnamese. Both assimilation and association, alternately considered fundamental to the French colonial presence in Indochina, remained notions rather than actualities, and the dream of a France in Asia could not be fulfilled.

NOTES

[1]Virginia Thompson, *French Indochina* (New York: Macmillan, 1937), p. 425.

[2]John F. Cady, *Southeast Asia: Its Historical Development* (New York: McGraw-Hill, 1964), p. 550.

[3]Great Britain, Naval Intelligence Division, *Indochina* (Cambridge: The University Press, 1943), p. 192.

[4]See: J. De Galembert, *Les Administrations et les services publics indochinois* (Hanoi: Imprimerie Mac Dinh Tu, 1931).

[5]Which comprised the colony of Cochinchina; the protectorates of Annam, Tongking, Cambodia, and Laos; and the leased territory of Kwang-chou-wan.

[6]Great Britain, *Indochina*, p. 198.

[7]For a full treatment of the administration and the procedures by which it worked, see De Galembert, *Les Administrations*.

[8]In 1925, most governmental activities were highly centralized, while the financial organization was decentralized. Until about 1927-28, when Varenne's fiscal reforms began to go into effect, there was great economic confusion for the colonial government.

[9]Camille Devilar, *Comment on perd une colonie* (Paris: Presses Modernes, 1927), p. 14.

[10]Cady, *Southeast Asia*, p. 547.

[11]Ibid., p. 554. The figures are Robequain's.

[12]Devilar, *Comment on perd*, p. 14.

[13]Or, at least, they considered politics among the Vietnamese, and opposition politics of any variety, undesirable.

[14]*Le Temps*, April 24, 1928.

[15]The figures for 1925 were almost identical.

See *L'Echo Annamite*, November 24, 1925.

[16]See below, pp. 107-108.

[17]Political irritants were usually summarily condemned and sent to Poulo Condore, a prison island off Cochinchina. The government was not always successful, however; the campaign to get rid of Paul Monin, Malraux's associate, for example, failed. See Walter G. Langlois, *André Malraux: The Indochina Adventure* (New York: Praeger, 1966), p. 61.

[18]Philippe Devillers, *Histoire du Viet-Nam de 1940 à 1952* (Paris: Editions du Seuil, 1952), p. 44.

[19]*L'Indochine*, June 18, 1925. Translation: Langlois, *André Malraux*, p. 64.

[20]Chester A. Bain, *The History of Vietnam from the French Penetration to 1939* (Ph.D. diss., The American University, 1956; Ann Arbor, University Microfilms, 1957), p. 513.

[21]Léon Werth, *Cochinchine* (Paris: Reider et Cie., 1926), p. 44.

[22]In 1910, three Frenchmen in Tongking could speak Vietnamese; 8 percent could get along in a restaurant, and 91 percent knew no Vietnamese at all (Bain, *The History*, p. 335). Doubtless, the situation had improved by 1925, but, judging from all accounts, not spectacularly.

[23]Often the feeling of having "lost Europe" was acute. One colonial said: "I suffer when I return to Europe. I find it hard to bear the twittering aimlessness of vacation. And above all I am disgusted by the ignorance of people at home . . . . They ask me questions like, 'Do you eat bread *(in Indochina)*? Do you have beds?'" (Werth, *Cochinchine*, p. 40).

[24]Ibid., p. 41.

[25]Devillers, *Histoire*, p. 44.

[26]D. G. E. Hall, *A History of Southeast Asia* (New York: Macmillan, 1958), p. 642. *Association* implied French and Vietnamese working together on an equal footing in and for a Vietnam that would benefit both. *Assimilation* promised to transform the Vietnamese into what would be, for all intents and

purposes, Frenchmen. The chief difficulty with assimilation as a policy was that it never was more
than a vague notion to which people became emotionally bound. Even those who bitterly opposed assimilation on the grounds that it was irrational, too
slow, or disruptive in its social effects, rarely
freed themselves from the basic concept of "civilizing" (read "Gallicizing") the Vietnamese. With such
thinking, *association* came to mean, in practice, the
coöperation of the French French and the Vietnamese
French, which presupposed much assimilation.

[27]Werth, *Cochinchine*, p. 131.

[28]Thompson, *French Indochina*, pp. 288-92.

[29]Bain, *The History*, p. 331, says the number
never exceeded five hundred. But see U.S. Department
of State, OIR Report #3708, *Political Alignments of
Vietnamese Nationalists* (Washington, 1949), pp. 157-
58, which notes that there were 631 students in 1937.

[30]*L'Echo Annamite*, September 24, 1926 (Varenne's
speech of September 19).

[31]Cady, *Southeast Asia*, p. 553.

[32]Thompson, *French Indochina*, p. 312.

[33]This is a moot point, actually, though all
sources speak of the free press in Cochinchina. It
was free in that papers existed and got away with
printing numerous unsavory things, but they existed
at the sufferance of the government and could be
persecuted at any time. Many of them were simply
more clever than the administration and published
despite it.

[34]For one example of how this happened, see
L'Indochine, July 8 and 24, 1925. Malraux calculated
convincingly that the administration not only supported six newspapers, to the tune of one and one-
half million francs each year, but that the head of
one newspaper, a close friend of the governor of
Cochinchina, Cognacq, made the equivalent of $70,000
from the operation.

[35]U.S. Department of State, *Political Alignments*, p. 8.

[36]Devilar, *Comment on perd*, p. 15.

[37]Ibid., p. 16.

[38]*Journal Officiel de l'Indochine*, September 9, 1925. Note erroneous citation in Devilar, *Comment on perd*, p. 16.

[39]Most of the foregoing biographical data is taken from *L'Echo Annamite*, August 1, 1925.

[40]*Argus Indochinoise*, November 18, 1925.

[41]Article from *La Montagne*, quoted in *L'Echo Annamite*, November 10, 1925.

[42]*La Cloche Fêlée*, December 3, 1925. The vote was 2,113 to 381.

[43]*L'Echo Annamite*, November 16, 1925. The original interview was held at the end of September.

[44]Ibid., November 12, 1925.

[45]Ibid., November 10, 1925.

[46]Devilar, *Comment on perd*, p. 16. Varenne was mocked, however, in *Canard Enchainée* (Paris), in an article titled "Why I wasn't chosen Governor-General of Indochina," quoted in *Argus Indochinoise*, December 2, 1925.

[47]From an interview given to Bùi Quang Chiêu in September (*L'Echo Annamite*, November 16, 1925).

[48]Quoted from *La Jeune République* (Paris), in *Argus Indochinoise*, December 12, 1925.

[49]*L'Echo Annamite*, November 16, 1925.

[50]*L'Indochine Enchainée*, November 25, 1925. Translation: Langlois, *André Malraux*, p. 162.

[51]Langlois, *André Malraux*, pp. 149-50.

[52]*L'Indochine*, June 22, 1925, and June 18, 1925.

[53]Full text in *Journal Officiel de l'Indochine*, November 14, 1925.

[54]See Devilar, *Comment on perd*, p. 65, and *L'Indochine*, August 6, 1925.

[55]*L'Indochine Enchainée*, November 28, 1925.

[56]Malraux's difficulties may be used as an example (see Langlois, *André Malraux*, passim,

especially pp. 145-62).

[57]*L'Indochine Enchaînée*, November 18, 1925.
Translation: Langlois, *André Malraux*, p. 165.

[58]Langlois, *André Malraux*, p. 83.

[59]*L'Echo Annamite*, November 19, 1925.

[60]See the decree on the subject, and details of
preparations, *L'Echo Annamite*, November 17, 1925.

[61]The Green Book report stated: "The policy of
the government of Cochinchina during the year that
has just ended has remained the same as the one followed during the three years preceding. Characterized by benevolence, it has aimed at the maintenance
of order, which is the essential factor for the peace
and prosperity of a country, but a prudent maintenance, obtained by conviction rather than by constraint" (Langlois, *André Malraux*, p. 173).

[62]*La Cloche Fêlée*, November 26, 1925.

[63]See *L'Echo Annamite*, November 28 to
December 4, 1925.

[64]In March 1926 (see advertisements in *L'Echo
Annamite*, March 25, 1926).

[65]*La Voix Libre*, November 28, 1925.

[66]*L'Indochine Enchaînée*, November 27 and 30,
1925.

[67]*La Voix Libre*, November 28, 1925.

[68]*L'Indochine Enchaînée*, November 27 and 30,
1925.

[69]*L'Echo Annamite*, November 30, 1925.

[70]*L'Indochine Enchaînée*, December 2, 1925.

[71]*La Cloche Fêlée*, December 3, 1925.

[72]*L'Echo Annamite*, December 30, 1925 (Varenne's
speech of December 20).

[73]Ibid., December 30, 1925.

[74]Ibid., December 30, 1925.

[75]See *Le Temps*, March 12, 1926.

[76]Varenne's letter is in *Le Temps*, March 23, 1926. On the incident and the culprit, see Devilar, *Comment on perd*, pp. 52ff.

[77]Devilar, *Comment on perd*, p. 26.

[78]See especially the biography contained in Nguyễn Phút Tân, *A Modern History of Vietnam* (Saigon: Khai Trí, 1964).

[79]Hoàng Văn Chi, *From Colonialism to Communism: A Case History of North Vietnam* (New York: Praeger, 1964), p. 18.

[80]*Argus Indochinoise*, December 5, 1925.

[81]Devilar, *Comment on perd*, p. 27.

[82]For example, buildings were searched very carefully before Varenne's arrival in Hanoi, and he was guarded extremely closely. Most observers agreed that the performance was to impress Varenne with the danger of bolshevism, and roundly denounced it (*L'Echo Annamite*, November 30, 1925).

[83]They were probably printed by enemies of Phan Bội Châu and of the Varenne administration (see *Argus Indochinoise*, December 19, 1925).

[84]*L'Echo Annamite*, December 11, 1925.

[85]Devilar, *Comment on perd*, pp. 27-28.

[86]The house arrest was not made clear by Varenne but was generally understood. The care with which the government watched Châu was not evident until December 2, 1926, when he was caught trying to escape for a visit to Hanoi. *L'Annam*, December 6, 1926, raised the question of whether the house arrest was legal under Indochinese regulations.

[87]I. Milton Sacks, "Marxism in Vietnam," in Frank N. Trager, ed., *Marxism in Southeast Asia* (Stanford: Stanford University Press, 1959), p. 117.

[88]U.S. Department of State, *Political Alignments*, p. 12.

[89]*L'Echo Annamite*, June 10, 1927.

[90] Ibid., November 21, 1925.

[91] Sacks, "Marxism," p. 113.

[92] *L'Echo Annamite*, November 16, 1925.

[93] Bùi Quang Chiêu in *Intransigeant* (Paris), quoted in *L'Echo Annamite*, November 7, 1925.

[94] *L'Echo Annamite*, January 8, 1920.

[95] Ibid., June 29, 1922.

[96] There were various ways, ranging from the use of the Sûreté to the prevention of copies of the newspaper's being sent through the mail.

[97] *L'Echo Annamite*, January 28, 1924.

[98] Ibid., February 13, 1924.

[99] That is, according to Malraux himself (see Langlois, *André Malraux*, p. 58). It is usually thought that the group was founded by Tạ Thu Thâu.

[100] *L'Annam*, May 20, 1926.

[101] *Argus Indochinoise*, August 1, 1925

[102] *La Cloche Fêlée*, January 14, 1924.

[103] Werth, *Cochinchine*, p. 138.

[104] *La Cloche Fêlée*, January 28, 1924.

[105] Werth, *Cochinchine*, p. 153.

[106] Quoted in Werth, *Cochinchine*, p. 162.

[107] *La Cloche Fêlée*, January 14, 1924.

[108] Quoted in Werth, *Cochinchine*, pp. 32-33.

[109] Phạm Quỳnh, *Essais Franco-Annamites (1929-1932)* (Huế: Editions Bùy-Huy-Tín, 1937), pp. 380-97, *passim*.

[110] Phạm Quỳnh, *Essais*, p. 190.

[111] Ibid., pp. 502-03.

[112] Ibid., p. 364.

113Ibid., p. 345.

114Ibid., p. 285.

115Ibid., p. 292.

116Ibid., p. 301.

117Ibid., p. 494.

118Ibid., p. 496.

119*La Cloche Fêlée*, January 7, 1924, and Werth, *Cochinchine*, pp. 32-33. Note Langlois's error, pp. 93ff, where he says the incident happened to Malraux.

120See, for example, Werth, *Cochinchine*, p. 124.

121Article from *L'Impartial* (Saigon), quoted in *La Presse Indochinoise*, July 20, 1924.

122Phạm Quỳnh, *Essais*, p. 291.

123Langlois, *André Malraux*, p. 57, and Thompson, *French Indochina*, p. 478.

124Phạm Quỳnh, *Essais*, pp. 286-87, quotes unknown author.

125Quoted in Werth, *Cochinchine*, p. 35.

126Giao quoted in *La Jeune République* (Paris), article reprinted in *Argus Indochinoise*, December 12, 1925.

127*La Cloche Fêleé*, March 22, 1926; restated in the following day's issue.

128Quoted and translated in Thomas E. Ennis, *French Policy and Development in Indochina* (Chicago: University of Chicago Press, 1936), p. 184.

129*La Cloche Fêlée*, April 8, 1926.

130Devilar, *Comment on perd*, pp. 73-75, gives a full account; other details appear in *L'Echo Annamite*, March 25, 1926.

131Thompson, *French Indochina*, p. 315.

132Cognacq was recalled in April 1926 and six months later was charged with serious administrative crimes. It was officially announced that he would not return to Indochina. See *L'Annam*, August 26, 1926.

[133]All sources consulted give Trinh's date of death as March 24; however, since Lâm Hiệp Châu's eulogy was written on March 23, a change might be called for, but see note 141.

[134]The text can be found in *Bulletin de l'Ecole Française d'Extrême Orient*, March-June 1907.

[135]Devillers, *Histoire*, p. 36.

[136]Cady, *Southeast Asia*, p. 558.

[137]See, for example, *Argus Indochinoise*, August 5, 1925.

[138]Quoted and translated in Langlois, *André Malraux*, p. 118.

[139]Ibid., p. 121, quoted and translated.

[140]Devilar, *Comment on perd*, p. 81, quotes Lachevrotière, who was, however, extremely biased in the affairs and may have fabricated these reasons.

[141]A possible explanation may be that Trinh was near death for several days previous to March 24. He had been bedridden since December 1925 (Nguyễn Phút Tan, *A Modern History*, p. 353).

[142]*Le Jeune Annam*, March 23, 1926.

[143]Devilar, *Comment on perd*, p. 81.

[144]Thompson, *French Indochina*, p. 295.

[145]Text in Devilar, *Comment on perd*, pp. 33-34.

[146]Thompson, *French Indochina*, p. 295.

[147]Bain, *The History*, p. 410.

[148]Ibid.

[149]*L'Echo Annamite*, October 2, 1926.

[150]Ibid., October 1, 1926.

[151]Ibid., October 1, 1926.

[152]Ibid., October 1, 1926. It is unclear whether Varenne thought that the early portion of his regime had represented tolerance or whether he considered his experiment to be as yet unstarted.

[153]Ibid., October 2, 1926.

[154]Ibid.

[155]Ibid., October 23, 1926.

[156]Ibid., October 27, 1926.

[157]Many sources say that Varenne refused, implying an official announcement. But he left Indochina for Paris on October 3, 1926, and there is no official notice in newspapers or the *Journal Officiel de l'Indochina,* which records all official acts.

[158]Ibid., October 14, 1926, quotes from *La Tribune Indochinoise.*

[159]*L'Annam*, November 25, 1926.

[160]*La Tribune Indochinoise*, November 5, 1926.

[161]See, for example, *L'Annam*, September 23, 1926, and *La Cloche Fêlée,* April 8, 1926.

[162]The radicals absorbed the Communist organization known as the Vietnam Revolutionary Youth League (Việt Nam Cách Mạnh Thanh Niên Hội) and changed their name to the New Vietnam Revolutionary party (Tân Việt Cách Mệnh Đảng) (U.S. Department of State, *Political Alignments*, pp. 17-18).

[163]*La Tribune Indochinoise,* November 10, 1926.

[164]Ibid., November 17, 1926.

[165]U.S. Department of State, *Political Alignments,* p. 33.

[166]Paul Isoart, *Le phenomène national Vietnamien* (Paris: Librairie générale de droit et de jurisprudence, 1961), p. 241.

[167]*L'Echo Annamite,* April 25, 1927.

THE FAITHFUL FEW: THE POLITICS OF COLLABORATION IN COCHINCHINA IN THE 1920s

By Milton Osborne

Those who chose to work with their foreign rulers in
the colonial period of Vietnamese history have consistently received less attention than their revolutionary countrymen who opposed French dominance. In
part, this neglect of the *collaborateurs*[1] stems from
the persistent historical preoccupation with success.
The collaborateurs failed to achieve their goals,
while the revolutionary nationalists finally succeeded in bringing the termination of French rule
over Vietnam. Another reason for neglect of the
collaborateurs, closely connected with that already
advanced, has been the difficulty for historians,
writing at a time when awareness of Vietnamese
nationalism is high, to reconcile the role of those
who worked for the French with any definition of
Vietnamese nationalism.[2] By being both unsuccessful
and historically unfashionable the collaborateurs
have in general not been the subject of deep study.
For the 1920s in Cochinchina, however, those collaborateurs who formed the loosely-knit political
group known as the Constitutionalist party have been
an exception. In a detailed and sympathetic article,
"Bùi Quang Chiêu and the Constitutionalist Party in

French Cochinchina, 1917-30," Dr. Ralph Smith has provided an account of the emergence of the Constitutionalists, of the principal goals which they pursued, and of their decline into political impotence.[3]

The present paper is not an attempt to cover the same ground as that trodden by Dr. Smith. It is, however, to a degree, a response to Dr. Smith's final comment in his article, in which he argues for the need to study the reasons for the Constitutionalists' failure. In making a call for such a study Dr. Smith appears to make the assumption that at the time of the Constitutionalist party was founded, and for a period during its existence as a political group, it was not unreasonable for its members to believe that their efforts to change, but not eliminate, French rule over Cochinchina had some chance of success. The present paper is written on the basis of a rather different assumption: that both because of the character of French rule in Cochinchina in the 1920s and because of the political program which they, themselves, espoused, the members of the Constitutionalist party at no stage were likely either to become the leaders of a significant political movement or to exert real influence on the formulation of French colonial policy. To hold such an assumption is not to discount the value of studying the Constitutionalist party and its leaders. Nor does such an assumption involve a judgment upon them of the sort provided by Joseph Buttinger, when he condemns the Constitutionalists for siding with the French administration at the time of the widespread and Communist-led agitation which took place in 1930.[4] The members of the Constitutionalist party were men of their time and reacted to events in accordance with standards in which they believed at that time. In this respect it is important to recognize a factor which has been largely neglected in the general historical literature on Vietnam during the 1920s and 1930s. This factor was the "tone" of life in the colonized society.[5] The record of French repression is well known in broad terms. An awareness of the details makes the hesitancy of collaborateurs such as the Constitutionalists to seek real change more understandable. At the same time, emphasis must be given to the manner in which they were unable to recognize the paradox involved in many of their most frequently promoted proposals. They proved incapable of perceiving the extent to which independence was indivisible.

In many ways those collaborateurs who were active in the Constitutionalist party during the

1920s were in an intellectual line of descent from
those Vietnamese who had joined their fortunes to
those of the French in the nineteenth century.
There is a striking similarity about a number of the
preoccupations of men such as Bùi Quang Chiêu, Nguyễn Phan Long, and Diệp Văn Cửởng during the 1920s
and the issues which concerned the more articulate
collaborateurs during the 1880s and 1890s.[6] The
collaborateur of the 1920s continued to focus much
of his political attention on such issues as the
need to advance "morality"--an ill-defined but nonetheless important concept, which seems to have owed
much to the continuing force of the Confucian ethic--
the desirability of extending and improving educational opportunities, and the problems associated
with the decline in importance of the traditional
Vietnamese commune. The pursuit of constitutional
political change was a new element in the set of
values held by the collaborateur element, but the
links with the past were significant in determining
their ultimate judgment that association with
France, at almost any cost, was the bedrock upon
which any foundation for political and personal
existence had to be laid.

     Yet the colony of Cochinchina, in which the
collaborateurs of the 1920s lived, was dominated by
an acute sense of fear on the part of the French

which, without doubt, had repercussions in the attitudes held by those who were the most important Vietnamese supporters of the colonial administration. Because of the need to rely upon official French sources in considering the 1920s, one may easily slip into the error of envisaging a political climate in which assured French colonial rulers governed their Vietnamese subjects, sustained by the conviction of their own omnipotence. This certainly is the picture which emerges from official records:

> The period between June 1921 and June 1922 was one of the most calm and satisfying ever known in Cochinchina.
>
> The influences, of an external origin, which could have worked in a pernicious manner upon persons of a weak or critical nature stopped of their own accord at our maritime frontiers and have not breasted our shores. Moreover, the personality of the Cochin-chinese is poorly disposed to the efforts of propagandists of subversive ideas....[7]

But, despite this official optimism, it is doubtful that a similar sense of underlying fear of the Viet-namese was matched in any other colonized Southeast Asian country at this time. The existence of the fear was seldom revealed explicitly. It was, how-ever, implicit and pervasive. One explanation for the existence of this fear may be found in the patriotic fervor evoked by World War I. In a way

164

experienced neither by the English nor by the Dutch
nations, the French suffered physically and spirit-
ually in that war. When the war began in 1914, the
French administration in Saïgon saw nothing strange
about their arranging for the composition and
circulation of patriotic songs and poems in Vietnamese for publication in newspapers. The correspond-
ence relating to these verses makes clear the assumption held by the French administrators that the
French struggle in Europe would be seen by a substantial number of Vietnamese in Cochinchina as their
struggle also.[8] Eighteen months later, as the war
dragged on and as frustration at the course of the
war bred ever greater concern and resentment, an
attack by members of a Vietnamese secret society on
the Saïgon Central Prison brought swift and terrible
French reaction. The lurking French fear of Vietnamese attack now appeared justified, and that attack had taken place in a time of war. Fifty-one
Vietnamese who had participated in the attack on
the prison were executed by firing squad, with the
leaders of the attacking group being forced to watch
while their followers were shot, six at a time,
before they, too, were executed.[9] The prospect of
further Vietnamese uprisings and the memory of this
Vietnamese "treachery" during the war appear to have
haunted the minds of Frenchmen, both official and

unofficial, in the years after 1918. Such a fear
was the justification for an extraordinary slaughter,
which took place even before the end of the war when
there was an attack upon French and Vietnamese prison
personnel on the island of Poulo Condore in April
1918. One Frenchman and two Vietnamese employees
of the administration were killed. In suppressing
this challenge, the French, in return, killed
seventy-five Vietnamese.[10]

The pervasive and deep nature of this fear
among Frenchmen in Cochinchina was reflected in the
reports which were carried in the Saïgon newspapers
of executions of Vietnamese who had been convicted
of crimes against Frenchmen. In *L'Opinion,* the
Courrier Saigonnais, and *L'Impartial* the details are
provided in an excruciating fashion. The account
of the execution itself is usually preceded by a
recapitulation of the crime for which the sentence
is being exacted. Then follows an account of the
mounting of the guillotine; the collection of the
condemned man from his cell, with an account of his
final *toilette* as the executioner shaves his neck;
note is taken of whether or not he drinks the brandy
customarily offered to him; and finally the scene at
the scaffold is described, even to the extent of
reporting the stench of blood when the blade has
fallen.[11]

The presence of the pervasive fear was a major
factor in bringing about the polarities in Vietnamese political participation which continued into the
revolutionary phase during the period after World
War II. In Cochinchina, at least, in the 1920s
there were only two choices for those who committed
themselves to any form of political action. Either
one was a collaborateur, within a range in which the
position of the Constitutionalists represented the
most radical endeavor, or one looked to the slowly
developing efforts of the revolutionaries, which
came, eventually, to be dominated by various Communist-led groups. Where fear drove the French
administration to reject any significant liberaliza-
tion of their rule, the middle ground of genuine
constitutional opposition of the sort which emerged
in India was not available. In stressing the existence of factors which eliminated the possibility of
a political middle ground, however, it is important
not to leave the impression that the collaborateurs
came to their political positions and advocated their
views purely in a reactive fashion. While the tone
of French colonial society led to polarization along
the lines just described, the decision in favor of
collaboration between French and Vietnamese was
clearly one which the collaborateur politicians had
reached as the result of conviction. Some considera-

tion of the individuals most prominent in the activities of the Constitutionalist party and of the goals which they pursued tends to elaborate this point.

Rather than repeat biographical details of the more prominent members of the Constitutionalist party, which have been published elsewhere,[12] there may be more value in providing some insight into the vision which these men held of themselves. In 1926, at the high point of their efforts to play a political role within the colony of Cochinchina, the appeal which they launched for support from the Vietnamese electorate for the Colonial Council was couched in these terms:

> Doctors, engineers, industrialists, businessmen, farmers, former civil servants, we present ourselves to the electoral college with the knowledge that we are not pursuing any personal advantage since each of us occupies in society a material and moral position which is able to assure us of a decent and independent existence.[13]

The Constitutionalists were, as they described themselves, men who did not lack material means. To the extent that information is available, there is no suggestion that the collaborateur element associated with the Constitutionalist party came from any one type of family background. Bùi Quang Chiêu was

168

descended from an old mandarin family, but Trần Văn
Don, another and younger member of the party, emerged
from much more humble circumstances.[14] Whatever
their family origins, however, certain personal
characteristics were held in common. These men were,
as I have mentioned, materially well established.
Whether professionally trained, like Bùi Quang Chiêu
and Dr. Trần Văn Đồn, or not, they had all received
a substantial amount of education in French--many
had passed through the most important of the secondary schools of the colony, the College Chasseloup-
Laubat in Saïgon. With their background of wealth,
education, and position they were convinced of their
own elite status and of the combined responsibilities
and privileges which accompanied it.

The strength of such a belief is graphically
revealed in a commentary written on political
developments in Cochinchina by Nguyễn Phan Long, the
man who, after Bùi Quang Chiêu, was probably the most
important member of the Constitutionalist party.
Writing in his newspaper, *L'Echo Annamite*, in 1922,
this former civil servant deplored the dangers of
allowing too many persons to participate in the
election of Vietnamese representatives to the Colonial Council of Cochinchina. Nguyễn Phan Long was
convinced that the new regulations which had been
introduced by the decree of June 9, 1922, which

increased the number of Vietnamese voters eligible
to cast votes for the ten Vietnamese members of the
council, had inherent dangers. By increasing the
size of the Vietnamese electoral college from less
than two thousand to about twenty thousand--in a
colony in which there were three million Vietnamese--
there was a grave risk of electoral corruption.
Nguyễn Phan Long's arguments were blunt and remarkably reminiscent of attitudes held by members of
the gentry in eighteenth-century England. Of the
twenty thousand Vietnamese entitled to vote, only
four thousand, in his estimation, could be classed
as well-to-do. Only such men, the argument ran, were
likely to resist pressure from the administration
or the temptation to accept bribes for their votes.
Indeed, it was Nguyễn Phan Long's conviction that a
considerable amount of vote-buying had taken place,
with corrupt village notables selling their votes.[15]

When the Constitutionalists put forth their
programs for action in Cochinchina, they either
failed to see, or were unable to see, the extent to
which these programs contained a basic paradox.
Their ultimate political goal was the achievement
of some ill-defined Cochinchinese independence from
France, but this autonomy was to be achieved through
Franco-Vietnamese collaboration. The acute nature
of this paradox is revealed by consideration of

political statements made by members of the party. The loyalty of the collaborateurs who made up the Constitutionalist party was to what they saw as the best in France and in Frenchmen. Since this was so, it was possible for members of the party to be quite sharply critical of the French in Cochinchina on occasion. Chafing at the unreadiness of the French administration to grant greater political rights to the Vietnamese, a writer in *L'Echo Annamite* for May 30, 1925, with the probably pseudonymous name of Đệ Tử (disciple), suggested that there had been greater material and moral progress in both Korea and Formosa under Japanese colonial control than there had been in Cochinchina under the French. There had, the writer went on in a satiric vein, been "progress" in Cochinchina:

> Consider the matter closely. Before the conquest there were virtually no brothels in the territory of the Annamese empire. Since then they have sprung up like mushrooms in all the European urban centers.
>
> There are facts which speak, and eloquently so.
>
> Mathematically, in this matter, civilization equals syphilization.
>
> Long live the speculum![16]

But along with criticism laced with such veneral allusions went a quite extraordinary readiness to

praise what was seen as the best in France and a
readiness to accept the existence of French "rights"
in Cochinchina. Indeed, Đệ Tử's article is less a
reflection of the general tone of the Constitutionalists' position than is Nguyễn Phan Long's commentary
on the problems of immigration into Cochinchina,
which he published in December 1922. In order to
understand the force of Long's comments one must
remember that the possibility of gaining French
naturalization was one of the most cherished goals
of the collaborateurs. The increasing reluctance of
the French authorities to permit Vietnamese in Cochinchina to gain the benefits of naturalization had
become a matter of resentment, and the pursuit of a
more liberal naturalization policy was an important
plank in the Constitutionalist party platform. The
issue was exacerbated by the fact that French subjects of Indian origin, born in such territories as
Pondicherry, did not face the same difficulties in
gaining French citizenship. These French Indian
subjects therefore were able to immigrate into Cochinchina, where, having gained citizenship, they
constituted an important voting bloc within the
French electoral college for the Colonial Council.
In complaining of this situation within the Colonial
Council, Nguyễn Phan Long went to great pains to
underline the point that his comments did not apply

172

to native Frenchmen, "les Français d'origine."
These men, Long noted, had, in addition to "those
other attributes common to all men--the right of
the victor, the prestige of the conqueror, the respect which is inspired by those people fulfilling
the role of the police *(all these attributes)* in the
eyes of a race *(the Vietnamese)* which has always
respected its masters."[17]

An important speech delivered by Bùi Quang
Chiêu in 1926 was less baldly subservient, but it
nonetheless leaves the clear impression that his
and his colleagues' view of the future was one in
which the continuing presence of France was an essential. Bùi Quang Chiêu had only just returned from a
visit to France, during which he had been unsuccessful in persuading the metropolitan authorities of
the necessity of making political reforms in Cochinchina. Upon his return he had encountered a demonstration of opposition to his policies from a conservative section of the French community in Saïgon
and a subsequent counterdemonstration from Vietnamese supporters of his position. Despite the failure
of his efforts in France, Bùi Quang Chiêu, speaking
on March 25 dressed in a dinner jacket and using
French rather than Vietnamese, referred to the
"sympathetic" reception which he had received in
France. Although his task remained incomplete, Bùi

Quang Chiêu expressed his conviction that "Annam and
France, united in a feeling of fraternal cooperation,
are capable of achieving great and beautiful things
in the Far East."[18] Two weeks later Bùi Quang Chiêu
made another notable speech in which he again lauded
the principle of Franco-Annamite collaboration as
"the basis of all native policy" in Cochinchina.[19]
The force of such a proposition, even with Bùi Quang
Chiêu's insistence that such collaboration would
involve the assumption of equality between the two
races, was undermined by his views, expressed in the
same speech, on the Nguyễn An Ninh affair. This
affair had involved the French administration's
prosecution of a young Vietnamese journalist for
publishing allegedly seditious material. This difficulty of the convinced collaborateur's position is
revealed in Bùi Quang Chiêu's comments on the case.
While ready to express his sympathy for Ninh, whose
actions stemmed from the lack of political progress
accorded the Vietnamese of Cochinchina by the
French, the admirer of that which is best in France
can only recommend that the law be allowed to take
its course.[20]

So far, emphasis has been placed on the general
paradox of the Constitutionalists' position, upon
their apparent failure to recognize the impossibility
of achieving any real measure of political autonomy,

so long as they were wedded to a political program
that called for close collaboration with a stronger
political entity which at no stage during the 1920s
showed any real inclination to grant the freedoms
which they sought. But the existence of this
general paradox should not distract attention from
some of the more particular contradictions within
their policies. The existence of these contradictions, or uncertainties, serves to illustrate the
fundamentally limited appeal of the Constitutionalists to Vietnamese society at large, and so to
emphasize the essentially restricted political con-
stituency from which they could expect support. I
have already alluded to the doubts which members of
the group held about the desirability of extending
political rights to those in the Vietnamese community
who did not enjoy the benefits of wealth. Their
views on education were similarly elite-oriented.
Nguyễn Phan Long, for instance, held strong reserva-
tions about the desirability of permitting too many
Vietnamese to study in France. Only a small number
of "subjects belonging to the elite" had received a
sufficient preparation, in his opinion, to permit
them to benefit fully from a period of study in
France.[21] His judgment was couched in practical
terms, but the underlying view of higher education
as the preserve of the few was also clearly present.

But it would be incorrect to leave the impression that the political impotence of the Constitutionalists, as the most interesting and active collaborateurs, stemmed solely from their failure to understand the paradoxical nature of many of their proposals. In the pursuit of their goals they faced political and economic difficulties which they could not surmount. One of these difficulties was the economic dominance of the Chinese in Cochinchina. During 1919 the organ of the Constitutionalist party, the *Tribune Indigène*, called for a Vietnamese boycott of Chinese businesses in Cochinchina, and efforts were made concurrently to establish Vietnamese-owned businesses, which could provide the services no longer sought from Chinese businessmen. After some limited success in the Saïgon-Cholon region, the boycott failed. There are various explanations which may be provided for this failure. One is that provided by Nguyễn Phan Long in *L'Echo Annamite* in 1922. According to this view, the boycott would have succeeded if it had lasted longer. The Chinese businessmen who were the objects of the boycott were, in Long's view, on their knees, and all that was required for success was a little more Vietnamese perseverance.[22] The view of the French was less sympathetic, but quite probably it is a more accurate assessment of the factors involved. In reports on

the efforts by the Constitutionalists to promote a
boycott, members of the French administration
stressed the relatively limited readership of those
newspapers which advocated the program and the
general indifference of the population to the idea.
As for Vietnamese members of the French administration, these men were still "much more interested in
preserving a trouble-free life than in involving
themselves in an agitation whose results seem to
them pretty problematical."[23]

The strength of Chinese commercial power in
Cochinchina and the reluctance of any large number
of Vietnamese to support the Constitutionalists'
boycott prevented the success of this policy. On
the issue of greater opportunities for naturalization, the aims of the Constitutionalists foundered
on the rock of French intransigence. This was an
issue which probably dismayed the collaborateurs more
than any other single policy failure.[24] As convinced advocates of the glory of France and as men
who had obtained naturalization themselves, they
deeply regretted the limitation which France placed
on the numbers of Vietnamese who were able to share
this benefit. A writer in *L'Echo Annamite* could
complain about the extent to which this limitation
on the number of naturalizations was seen as a
"gesture of disdain and of suspicion which is not

merited, for it repulses the natives who, drawn by the light which shines from her *(France)*, come to her under the impetus of admiration and love."[25] Such effusions were of little importance to an administration which had set its face against any rapid increase in naturalizations because of the possible political risks involved in extending too widely the political freedoms that were associated with French citizenship. In 1925, despite the continuing call for greater readiness to extend naturalization, the total number of persons naturalized in Cochinchina was thirty-one.[26]

In the face of the disappointments which they sustained, the continued readiness to work with the French of the collaborateurs who made up the membership of the Constitutionalist party requires explanation. Any simple answer which stressed their material interest in the continuing effectiveness of French rule would fail to come to grips with what is, perhaps, the most striking aspect of the political position adopted by these men.[27] There can be no doubt that these collaborateurs pursued their policies because they believed in them. In short, they were collaborateurs by conviction. The existence of such a conviction about the value of Franco-Vietnamese collaboration appears to have been closely linked with their political philosophy, an

amorphous but important series of attitudes linked
with their view of Vietnam's place in the world. It
is impossible to give this set of beliefs or assump-
tions any single satisfactory name or to describe it
in any very precise fashion. One fundamental belief
within the more general web of beliefs was that in
some manner Vietnam had lost its way or--to seek
another way of expressing this idea--that Vietnam
had been prevented from fulfilling its historical
destiny. I have suggested that one can trace an
intellectual line of descent between collaborateurs
of the sort to be found in the Constitutionalist
party and those earlier collaborateurs who had chosen
to work with the French in the first few decades
of the French presence in Vietnam. The validity of
this assertion is underlined if consideration is
given to the views expressed by Trương Vĩnh Ký in
the nineteenth century and those stated by Nguyễn
Phan Long in the 1920s. Repeatedly during the 1870s
and 1880s, Trương Vĩnh Ký, one of the earliest and
most distinguished of the collaborateurs during conquest and immediately afterward, praised the opportunity which French colonial occupation of Vietnam
gave for transforming a "disinherited country" and a
"decaying nation."[28] Trương Vĩnh Ký held to this
view until his death in 1898. In 1923 one finds a
striking similarity in the views expressed by Nguyễn

Phan Long. Addressing a group of visiting members
of the French parliament, he drew attention to the
state of the Vietnamese population. They had been
delivered from mandarinal oppression, Nguyễn Phan
Long noted, by the onset of French colonial power,
but they still had to come to terms with the striking
force of new, Western ideas. In his view it was
France's duty to save the Vietnamese people from
"this decadence of a race which has passed into a
slow and sweet state of dying, this twilight of a
people whose spiritual death has the morbid charm of
a sunset."[29]   It was the conviction that France alone
could provide Vietnam with its necessary transformation which led Bùi Quang Chiêu to praise the great
nineteenth-century mandarin Phan Thanh Giản as "this
first friend of France, he to whom we owe the joy of
collaborating...."[30]

In granting the existence of conviction as an
explanation of the positions adopted by the collab-
orateurs--and there were many who sought less
political change than the Constitutionalists--one
must still judge them to have been surprisingly
unperceptive in their inability to recognize that
France never showed any real inclination during the
1920s to share power in the fashion that they advocated. The collaborateurs either failed genuinely
to recognize that this would be so, or they became

180

prepared to accept less. There are dangers in emphasizing the latter position, since, as convinced
admirers of the French, most of the collaborateurs
would have shared the fears of the French about the
dangers of revolution, which from 1929 and 1930
onward appeared increasingly likely to undermine
French rule in Vietnam. The year 1930 was probably
vital in blunting whatever was critical in their
view of the French role in Cochinchina. Not only
was 1930 the year of sustained Communist-led agitation against French rule in north-central Annam,
particularly in the province of Nghệ-An, but it was
also a year of unprecedented agitation in Cochinchina. And 1930 was a year of near-hysteria among the
French community in Vietnam concerning the dangers
of communism. For the wealthy, elitist members of
the collaborateur community, the threat of communism
was a matter for concern also, and it is notable
that expressions of opinion early in 1930 which
criticised the level of force used by the French
to suppress agitation in Annam, became increasingly
muted as the agitation continued through the year.[31]
Communism was, of course, an important threat to the
continuing power of the French, but it was attitudes
like those held by the collaborateurs which helped to
make it so. They were an elitist group. Whatever
political aims some, such as the Constitutionalists,

181

pursued, they were a group committed to maintaining the French in power. And they failed to recognize why communism could have an appeal to the peasantry of Vietnam.

In an attempt to explain the inability, or the unreadiness, of men like Bùi Quang Chiêu and Nguyễn Phan Long to recognize the paradox of their position, one further factor should probably be cited. This was the persistent, and, at times, bitter criticism which these men and their supporters had to sustain in the course of their political careers from the outspoken and conservative colon element in Cochinchina. Almost from the beginning of their political endeavors, Bùi Quang Chiêu and his associates came under sharp criticism for their policies. An exchange between the Constitutionalist *Tribune Indigène* and the, at that stage, pro-colon newspaper *L'Opinion* makes this point. In an article of May 10, 1919, Bùi Quang Chiêu in the *Tribune Indigène* argued that the Constitutionalists' attempts to get a constitution for Cochinchina did not represent an effort to achieve political independence from France. An editorial in *L'Opinion* for May 11/12, 1919, condemned Chiêu's claim as an example of his hypocrisy. Bùi Quang Chiêu was accused of making "Bolshevik calculations," which deprived him of "any right to our pity." Criticism of this sort continued over the years, frequently led by a French journalist and colonial politician, Lachevrotière. It was this journalist who in 1930 accused the Constitutionalists of being behind the agitation which developed in Cochinchina.[32] And it was the same journalist who, following the electoral successes of the Constitutionalists in 1926, spared no effort to insult and embarrass them in the Colonial Council.[33] It may be possible to exaggerate the effect of the continued criticisms and insults which the collaborateur politicians had to endure during their careers; nevertheless, the existence of this long record of criticism may be judged to have had some political effect. Nothing could be more galling for the convinced advocate of Franco-Vietnamese collaboration than to find himself to be the target of abuse from Frenchmen. One way to deal with the problem would have been to abandon belief in the possibility of cooperation. Another approach would have been to avoid committing oneself to positions which were likely to bring further barbs. In the emotionally charged atmosphere of the early 1930s there were few among the collaborateurs who were ready to risk any extended exposure to the slings and arrows of outrageous French opinion.[34]

Given their failure to achieve any significant gains, the Constitutionalists might seem to repre-

sent, essentially, a footnote to the history of
Vietnam. Such a view neglects the fact that many of
the views on the desirability of Franco-Vietnamese
collaboration held by the Constitutionalists, in
particular, and the collaborateur element, in general,
persisted throughout the 1930s and into the 1940s.
Furthermore, such a view fails to take account of the
way in which the views and attitudes which have been
described in this paper were held by Vietnamese in
Tongking and Annam, as well as in Cochinchina. Dr.
Ralph Smith, in his review of the Constitutionalists,
has drawn attention to the similarity in views between the Constitutionalists and the northern Vietnamese journalist Phạm Quỳnh.[35] Another, and one
of the most striking, statements in favor of Franco-
Vietnamese collaboration to be published in the 1930s
is one that may be found in the Hanoï newspaper
La Patrie Annamite. In five long articles with the
general heading "Vers une doctrine nationale" a
writer identified only by the initials P. A. presents
as developed and coherent a statement on the virtues
of Franco-Vietnamese collaboration as is to be found
in the literature of the colonial period during the
twentieth century.[36] In brief, an understanding of
developments in Vietnam in the 1920s and 1930s must
take account of attitudes which, however unfashionable
they may appear today, represented one of the sig-

184

nificant reactions to the French colonial presence.

Early in this paper the suggestion was made that what was surprising about the Constitutionalists was not the fact that they failed, but rather that they should have expected to succeed. Caught in the paradox of their own political position and faced with the unwillingness of the French administration to make any significant concession, there seems considerable justification for the estimation that their efforts were doomed from the start. It is possibly unfair to tax a collaborateur such as Nguyễn Phan Long with failing to recognize the potential appeal of communism to the Vietnamese when he commented on "bolshevism" in 1921. At that time there was little reason for any observer to envisage the eventual role which the Vietnamese Communist party was to play in Vietnamese politics. There is, nevertheless, a strong streak of irony in the views which he expressed about the Congress of Tours, where, as he put it, "an Annamite, who represented himself as a delegate of the Indochinese Communist group vehemently attacked, in the slang dear to those who are contemptuous of bourgeois regimes, the evils of capitalism, aggravated by abuses which could be blamed on the French administration in this country. These complaints have had no echo in Indochina, their violent nature has brought forth smiles. It is time to repeat the proverb 'One swallow does not make spring.'"[37] The Vietnamese to whom Nguyễn Phan Long was referring was, of course, Hồ Chí Minh.

NOTES

Much of the research necessary for this paper was carried out in Saigon as part of a research project financed by the Australian Research Grants Committee. The writer gratefully acknowledges the support given by the ARGC, but emphasizes that he alone bears responsibility for the statements made and the views expressed in this paper.

[1]As in *The French Presence in Cochinchina and Cambodia: Rule and Response (1859-1905)* (Ithaca, N. Y.: Cornell University Press, 1969) the French word *collaborateur* is used here to avoid the opprobrious associations attached to the english word *collaborator*. For the collaborateur element in Vietnamese colonial society the concept of working with the French authorities--that is, of *collaboration*--was something admirable.

[2]Some of the issues raised here are discussed in my "Trương Vĩnh Ký and Phan Than Giản: The Problem of a Nationalist Interpretation of Nineteenth-Century Vietnamese History," *Journal of Asian Studies* vol. 30, no. 1 (November 1970), pp. 81-93.

[3]*Modern Asian Studies* vol. 3, no. 2 (1969), pp. 131-150. The same author's *Viet-Nam and the West* (London, 1968) gives some account of the Constitutionalists in a more general review of Vietnamese history.

[4]Joseph Buttinger, *Vietnam: A Dragon Embattled*, 2 vols. (New York: Praeger, 1967), 1:202.

[5]Walter J. Langlois' *André Malraux: The Indochinese Adventure* (London, 1966) is one of the rare scholarly books which does provide an insight into the character of French colonial society in Vietnam in a detailed fashion.

[6]The role and the preoccupations of the Vietnamese collaborateurs in Cochinchina during the first forty to fifty years of French rule are examined in some detail in my *The French Presence in Cochinchina and Cambodia*.

[7]*Indochine Française, Rapports au Conseil du Gouvernement* (Session ordinaire de 1922), Rapport sur la situation de Cochinchine, p. 193.

187

[8]Archives of the Republic of Vietnam, S.L.2,009 letter from M Helgoual'ch to the governor of Cochinchina, Saïgon, August 24, 1914. This dossier contains the quốc-ngữ text of the verses with such titles as "Chúc Pháp-Quấc Tịnh Chư Liên Quấc Ca" (Homage to France and Her Allies).

[9]*L'Opinion* (Saïgon), 23 February 1916, contains a long account of this affair. The Vietnamese who were executed were not tried before a civil court but by a military council of war.

[10]*L'Opinion*, April 14/15, 18 and 19.

[11]These comments are made after perusal of a wide range of newspapers published throughout the 1920s. One particularly notable instance of the type of account just described is that to be found in *L'Opinion* for January 29, 1929, where an account is provided of the execution of Trần Duy Tự for his part in the murder of a French plantation manager in September 1927.

[12]Considerable detail on Bùi Quang Chiêu is provided by R. B. Smith in "Bùi Quang Chiêu and the Constitutionalist Party in French Cochinchina, 1917-30." In the same article Dr. Smith summarizes the available information on such men as Nguyễn Phan Long and Diệp Văn Cường. Some discussion of the significance of Bùi Quang Chiêu in relation to the collaborateur element of the nineteenth and early twentieth centuries is to be found in *The French Presence in Cochinchina and Cambodia*, pp. 142, 160, and 279.

[13]*L'Opinion*, September 30, 1926. The statement was signed by the complete slate of Constitutionalist candidates for the Colonial Council: Bùi Quang Chiêu, Huỳnh Ngọc Bỉnh, Lê Quang Liêm (known as Bảy), Nguyễn Phan Long, Nguyễn Tấn Được, Nguyễn Văn Huợt, Ngô Văn Huân, Nguyễn Văn Thinh, Trần Văn Đốn, and Trương Văn Bến.

[14]I am indebted to Trần Văn Đốn's son, the former General Trần Văn Đốn, for information on his father. Trần Văn Đốn, the elder, was sponsored in his early childhood by a Frenchman who was impressed by the young boy's interest in learning. This interest culminated in Trần Văn Đốn's completing his medical studies in France.

[15]*L'Echo Annamite* (Saïgon), November 9, 1922.

[16]The reaction of the European press in Cochinchina to such an article is readily imagined. In *L'Opin-*

ion for June 10, 1925, the comment was made that "it is a characteristic of petty minds and of monkeys to denigrate everything without admiring anything."

[17]*L'Echo Annamite*, December 12, 1922.

[18]*L'Opinion*, March 26, 1926.

[19]Ibid., April 12, 1926.

[20]Ibid., April 12, 1926. Nguyễn An Ninh was prosecuted for material published in the pamphlet *La France en Indochine*, extracts from which can be found in *L'Opinion*, September 11, 1925.

[21]*L'Echo Annamite*, August 1, 1922.

[22]July 6, 1922.

[23]Archives of the Republic of Vietnam, S.L.343 "Rapport politique du 3me trimestre 1919," Saigon, November 29, 1919, signed Maspero, Governor p.i. of Cochinchina, No. 750 S.L.364 "Rapport politique du 4me trimestre 1919," Saïgon, 19 March 1920, signed Le Gallen, Governor of Cochinchina, No. 160. S.L.365 "Rapport politique du 4me trimestre 1920," Saïgon, unsigned, undated, and unnumbered. The quotation is from dossier S.L.365.

[24]See *La Tribune Indigène* of June 29, 1923, for an indication of the Constitutionalists' feelings on the matter.

[25]*L'Echo Annamite*, July 2, 1921.

[26]The figure is given in *L'Opinion* July 7, 1926. No breakdown of the previous legal status of those involved is provided. On the basis of earlier examples, however, it seems safe to conclude that some of the thirty-one persons involved were not Vietnamese. The number of Vietnamese naturalized in 1925 was thus likely to have been even fewer than thirty-one.

[27]The point is *not* that the Constitutionalists can be seen to have had no material interest in the continuance of the French regime in Cochinchina. As men of substance they were not in favor of a Socialist revolution. But emphasis on a crudely venal aspect of their views distorts their clearly genuine belief in the possibility of Franco-Vietnamese cooperation--at least, up to 1926.

[28]See *The French Presence in Cochinchina and*

Cambodia, pp. 97-98, for quotations from Ký's writings and some discussion of this question.

[29]Long was speaking as the representative of the "elite annamite"; his speech is reported in *L'Opinion*, February 14, 1923.

[30]*L'Opinion*, November 15, 1928.

[31]See, for instance, the commentary on events at Yên Báy by Dưởng Văn Lợi in *L'Echo Annamite*, March 12 and 19, 1930.

[32]For some discussion of this accusation, see *L'Echo Annamite*, June 7 and 16, 1930. There is considerable irony in this accusation, since Bùi Quang Chiêu and Nguyễn Phan Long were objects of attack in tracts distributed by those seeking to foment agitation against French rule in Cochinchina in 1930. *L'Opinion*, June 17, 1930, quotes from one of these tracts, which states, "At the moment when all the compatriots are resolutely working for the general benefit, the Nguyễn Phan Longs and the Bùi Quang Chiêus and their acolytes are acting as hunting dogs for the administration in order to wreck our efforts."

[33]See *L'Opinion*, November 16, 1926, for the incidents which accompanied the opening of the sessions of the Colonial Council.

[34]Perhaps not surprisingly, but nonetheless strikingly, the French administration was consistently unsympathetic in its attitudes toward the collaborateurs. It was not merely the collaborateurs' political aims which attracted criticism, but also their life-style. One finds men like Bùi Quang Chiêu being referred to as *néo-occidentaux* in official French reports. See Archives of the Republic of Vietnam, S.L.364, "Rapport politique du 4me trimestre 1919," Saïgon, March 19, 1920, signed by Le Gallen, Governor of Cochinchina, No. 160.

[35]"Bùi Quang Chiêu and the Constitutionalist Party in French Cochinchina, 1917-30," 142-143.

[36]The articles commence in *La Patrie Annamite*, April 20, 1935.

[37]*L'Echo Annamite*, September 15, 1921.

QUỐC NGỮ AND THE DEVELOPMENT OF
MODERN VIETNAMESE LITERATURE

By Hoàng Ngọc Thành

Booming everywhere is gunfire,
Smoke spreads and obscures the ground,
Burning fire lights the clouds.[1]

Such is the way Mrs. Nguyễn Nhược Thị, in her poem
"Hạnh Thục Ca," describes the fight in the capital
of Huế between the Vietnamese and the French on the
night of July 5, 1885, and the subsequent occupation
of the city by French troops. A new page of Vietnamese history had been turned: Vietnam lost her
independence and was subjected to French domination.
It was the culmination of a long process of Western
encroachment and imperialism, begun in the 1840s,
which the kings of the Nguyễn dynasty (1802-1945) and
the Vietnamese Confucian scholar class could not
successfully resist.

PART I

The French first established themselves in Cochinchina in the 1860s. This area had only been recently

settled by the Vietnamese. When it became a colony under direct French administration and laws, the traditional civil service examinations were abolished right away, and schools were opened to teach French and *quốc ngữ*, the romanized script of spoken Vietnamese. Modern printing was introduced, and the publication of books in quốc ngữ was encouraged. As far back as 1865, only two years after the occupation of the three eastern provinces of Cochinchina, the French-sponsored *Gia Định Báo* (Newspaper of Gia Dinh) was published in quốc ngữ.[2]

Indeed, quốc ngữ had been invented and put into final form by many Italian, Portuguese, French, and Spanish missionaries, who wanted an easier system of writing than Chinese characters or the *chữ nôm*, a script using combinations and modifications of Chinese characters for writing non-Chinese Vietnamese words. Among these missionaries a French priest, Alexandre de Rhodes (1591-1660), had made the greatest contribution to the formation of quốc ngữ with his production of the first prayer book in Latin and quốc ngữ and his publication of the *Relazione de filici successi della fede nel regno di Tunchino* in 1650 and a Vietnamese-Portuguese-Latin dictionary, the *Dictionarium annamiticum, lusitanum et latinum*, in 1651.[3] For the first time the Vietnamese spoken language was systematically reproduced

192

in the Latin alphabet, with accent marks taken from
the Portuguese to indicate the Vietnamese six tones.
Quốc ngữ was at first used for Christian proselytiz-
ing. Prayer books were published in quốc ngữ for
the Christian Vietnamese, who were taught this
romanized script. So from the late seventeenth
century to the 1860s quốc ngữ had been the language
of Christian missions in their work with the Vietnamese Catholic minority.

  With the coming of the French to Cochinchina in
the 1860s, missionaries acquired liberty of worship
and French protection. Christian converts increased
in number. More books in quốc ngữ were printed.
At first they were printed at Serampore, India, or
Bangkok, Thailand, and then taken to Saigon.[4] But
soon they were printed in Saigon. A number of pamphlets, poems, plays, and stories having Christian
content were produced, which, besides serving their
religious purposes, contributed to the dissemination
of quốc ngữ.[5] Schools were established. In 1885,
for instance, three schools for interpreters opened
in Saigon to train native interpreters in French
and quốc ngữ. The French authorities promoted the
learning of quốc ngữ for many reasons. Quốc ngữ is
easier to learn than Chinese characters, and French
administrators who learned it could thus exercise
control over Vietnamese publications. Quốc ngữ was

also a convenient writing system for the administration of the country. And quốc ngữ, by teaching Vietnamese the roman script, could help introduce the Vietnamese to the French language and thus to French culture and literature, thereby severing the links of the indigenous people with their own cultural past, preserved in Chinese characters and chữ nôm. Gradually quốc ngữ became the national written language of the Vietnamese, an efficient cultural tool for their advancement. The Vietnamese in Cochinchina, Christian and non-Christian, were the first to study quốc ngữ. The first well-known writers in quốc ngữ were two Catholic southerners, Huỳnh Tịnh Của (1834-1907) and Trương Vĩnh Ký (1837-98).

Huỳnh Tịnh Của was a Confucian scholar who, besides being fluent in Chinese, knew French and quốc ngữ fairly well. He was placed in charge of the translation of judicial papers for the colonial government of Cochinchina. He was also the editor of the first newspaper in quốc ngữ, the *Gia Định Báo*. He wrote the first dictionary of Vietnamese, a book on proverbs and popular sayings, and *Stories for Fun,* a collection published in two volumes in 1880 and 1885.[6] This collection has a hundred twelve stories, one to two pages long. They have Chinese settings; they are amusing, but they also contain

moral implications which denote the Confucian out-
look and Chinese cultural background of the author.[7]
The quốc ngữ in this collection is quite simple and
uses many common words.

The second writer, Trương Vĩnh Ký, was a great
scholar in his own right. A graduate of the Catholic
missionary schools of Pinhalu in Cambodia and Penang
in Malaysia, Ký knew many languages. Besides French
and Chinese, in which he was fluent, he also had
some knowledge of Cambodian, Laotian, Thai, Burmese,
Japanese, Hindi, Greek, Latin, and English. In 1863
he served as interpreter for the Vietnamese embassy
of Phan Thanh Giản to the court of Napoleon III. In
1884, the French administration appointed him
instructor at the College des Stagiaires and the
College of Interpreters in Saigon. He was also an
editor of the *Gia Định Báo*. He produced over a
hundred works including French-Vietnamese/Vietnamese-
French dictionaries, books on Vietnamese history,
and booklets on the study of quốc ngữ and foreign
languages. He translated the Chinese classics into
quốc ngữ. Ký contributed greatly to the dissemination and popularization of quốc ngữ. With his
voluminous literary production, he showed that quốc
ngữ could be used to express any subject, philosophical or literary. A very interesting aspect of his
work is his translation of many traditional novels

from chữ nôm into quốc ngữ; such as *Truyện Kiều* in
1875, *Lục Súc Tranh Công* in 1887, and *Phan Trần* in
1889.[8] By translating these works into quốc ngữ,
Trương Vĩnh Ký provided a bridge between the past
and the future, between traditional Vietnam and a
new Vietnam emerging under alien rule. People who
knew quốc ngữ could now enjoy traditional literary
masterpieces without studying Chinese characters or
chữ nôm. Ký also authored two small volumes of
short stories similar to the *Stories for Fun* by
Huỳnh Tịnh Của, the *Ancient Stories* in 1866 and the
Humorous Stories in 1882.[9] These stories have a
more indigenous, native character in setting and
content than those by Huỳnh Tịnh Của. Many are
entertaining, such as those concerning Dr. Quỳnh, a
learned fictional figure, who laughed at and fooled
many people. Most, however, also have a moral meaning and provide the reader with good and bad examples
in life and society.[10] These two volumes of stories
have been very popular and widely read.

Gradually, quốc ngữ gained ground in Cochinchina, with the endorsement and encouragement of the
colonial authorities and also because of the work of
writers such as Huỳnh Tịnh Của and Trương Vĩnh Ký.
In 1901 a second newspaper in quốc ngữ, *Nông Cổ Mín
Đàm,* was published in Saigon.

In the central and northern area--in Annam and

Tongking--French authorities proceeded more cautiously in the cultural field. The traditional civil-service examinations were maintained until 1915 in Tongking and 1918 in Annam. But in 1906 the teaching of quốc ngữ was made compulsory in the village and provincial schools. French became one of the subjects in the traditional examinations.[11] Subjects such as Western history, general science, and the geography of the country were introduced, and examination papers were given grades of from 0 to 20, in the European fashion.[12]

PART II

A gradual evolution of Vietnamese society was clearly to be perceived. By 1900, except for the struggle led by Hoàng Hoa Thám, with whom the French authorities had to negotiate and to whom they conceded the Yên Thế base, movements of resistance had been subdued. The harshness of the pacification effort is related in the writings of many French military and civilian authorities of the time.[13] Although effective armed opposition to the French had come to an end, the people still showed their opposition to foreign rule. In fact, until the end of the French domination on March 9, 1945, there continued to be sporadic armed uprisings, demonstrations, and terrorist acts, as well as speeches and tracts against the colonial authorities. Even in Cochinchina, where French colonization had been established for almost forty years, the common people recited long poetic stories in the 6-8 meter relating the activities of anti-French resistance leaders like Quảng Hớn, Thông Chánh, and Sáu Trọng.[14] Many patriotic poems, such as the very well known Á tế Á (Asia), were disseminated among the masses and were recited and memorized by many people. Á tế Á is a story, written in poetic form by an anonymous author, about Western imperialism in Asia and the modernization of Japan. It denounces French colonialism and calls upon the Vietnamese to build a new culture, to be united for the development of commerce, for freedom.[15] The more the Vietnamese knew how to read and write in quốc ngữ, which became the vehicle for instruction of the common people, the more the Vietnamese became educated and learned from the West, the more they opposed alien rule.

Quốc ngữ was gaining acceptance even among the Confucian scholars. Indeed, the Confucian scholars, realizing more and more the weakness of their traditional learning, began to see their engrossment in Confucian study as a cause of their defeat at the hands of the French. They concluded that they had to

seek new knowledge and techniques. Knowing Chinese
well, they came into contact with Chinese writings
published in the last decades of the nineteenth and
the first of the twentieth centuries. They got to
know, through Chinese translations, such Western
philosophers as Socrates, Plato, Aristotle, Bacon,
Descartes, Montesquieu, Rousseau, Voltaire, Darwin,
Adam Smith, and Spencer and famous persons such as
Joan of Arc, Madame Roland, Peter the Great, and
Napoléon. They read about such strange names as
Mazzini, Garibaldi, and Cavour in Italy and Saigo
Takamori, Fukuzawa Yukichi, and Yoshida Shoin in
Japan, the "six reformers" who were executed after
the failure of "the hundred days of reform" in China,
and Aguinaldo in the Philippines.[16] They admired
Bismarck and Moltke for their victories over the
French. A new kind of knowledge, very much dif-
ferent from what they had known so far, opened new
horizons for them. They understood the tremendous
advance of the West in technology, in material
achievements, and in progressive ideas. They were
influenced by the writings of the Chinese reformists
K'ang Yu-wei and Liang Ch'i-ch'ao. The victory of
Japan over Russia in the 1904-05 war convinced them
that Western ideas and technology--in brief,
Westernization--were necessary steps toward their own
salvation. Hence, there developed a movement for

study abroad, an "exodus toward the East." Under
the encouragement of the Confucian-scholar-turned-
revolutionary Phan Bội Châu and the royal prince
Cường Để, many young men left the country secretly
to study in China and, especially, in Japan.[17] Phan
Bội Châu can be considered the most famous Vietnamese
revolutionary of the first two decades of the twentieth century. In 1902 he produced "Letters Written
in Blood from Abroad," describing the national
humiliation and loss of independence, in order to
raise the patriotic feelings of the people. Châu
traveled widely, carrying on his anti-French activities in Thailand, China, and Japan. He met Liang
Ch'i-ch'ao, Sun Yat-sen, Okuma, and Inukai, among
others. He also wrote "New Letters in Blood from
Abroad" in 1906 and a "History of the Loss of Independence of Vietnam." In Tokyo he founded the
Association for the Modernization of Vietnam, the
League for the Restoration of Vietnam, and a government in exile with Prince Cường Để. Most of Phan
Bội Châu's writings were in Chinese, but they were
translated into quốc ngữ. They were propagated
illegally and secretly among the people and had a
strong influence.

Besides absorbing new ideas from the West, the
Vietnamese also began to adopt a number of Western
ways of life. Many aspects of traditional society

200

underwent a gradual transformation. Confucian
scholars began to realize the backwardness of a
number of their customs. Typical was the movement
to cut hair short in the Western way. In 1905 a
scholar and former mandarin of the court of Huế,
turned reformist, Phan Châu Trinh, and another
scholar, Nguyễn Quyền, cut off their traditional
chignons. Thousands of people in the cities and
the countryside followed their example. The haircut
movement showed the Vietnamese eagerness to adopt
modern ways of life and certainly had political
implications.[18]

These longings for modernization, for independence, were clearly expressed in the opening of
the Tongking School of the Righteous Cause[19] in
March 1907. It was sponsored by many Confucian
scholars, among them Nguyễn Quyền, former đốc học
(inspector of studies) of the province of Lạng Sơn,
who had received a one-year leave of absence from
the colonial authorities. The Tongking School of
the Righteous Cause had on its staff such Confucian
scholars who had turned reformists or revolutionaries
as Phan Châu Trinh, Lương Văn Can, Tăng Bạt Hổ, and
Lương Trúc Đàm, and graduates of French schools such
as the interpreter-newsman Nguyễn Văn Vĩnh. It had
the objective of modernizing the country through
education and economic development. It was opposed

to traditional learning, and it taught practical subjects such as science, foreign languages, history, and geography. Teaching was conducted in three languages--Vietnamese, French, and Chinese. It had its own printing press, which issued pamphlets and booklets on basic scientific knowledge. It also criticized backward customs and superstitions and promoted the wearing of European clothes, made with local material. The school also engaged in economic activities. Within a few weeks after its opening, the school had over a thousand students of both sexes learning together, which was quite an innovation for Vietnam at the beginning of the twentieth century and a radical departure from the Confucian concept of separation of sexes. Many branches of the school were established in Cochinchina, in central Vietnam, and in the province of Nghệ An. The Tongking School of the Righteous Cause appeared to symbolize the aspirations of the Vietnamese people for modernization and emancipation.

To counteract the influence of the school and the scholars who proposed it, colonial authorities opened a number of schools to teach French and quốc ngữ, such as the Tân Quy School. A Franco-Vietnamese library was opened in Hanoi.[20] The French also announced the opening of a so-called University of Hanoi. But the influence of the Tongking School for the Righteous Cause kept growing. The French authorities became so worried that they closed it in December 1907.

Closing the Tongking School, however, proved to be no solution, and the political situation in Vietnam in the years preceding World War I became increasingly tense. In March and April 1908 peasants in the provinces of Quảng Ngãi, Bình Định, and Thừa Thiên, wearing short clothes instead of the traditional long, black tunics and with short hair, held demonstrations against heavy taxes. The French repressed them brutally. Shooting demonstrators, burning houses, and arresting masses of people became regular practices. Accused by the French and collaborationist administration of having incited the peasants, some Confucian scholars suffered execution, and others imprisonment or exile. Among them, a doctor of letters, Trần Quý Cáp, inspector of studies of the province of Khánh Hòa, was executed twenty hours after his arrest without trial or serious proof. The reformist Phan Châu Trinh was condemned to death and then exiled to Poulo Condore island. In June an attempt was made to poison the French garrison of Hanoi. The colonial government reacted by closing the so-called University of Hanoi for "lack of students."

The French, however, continued to give some support to education, for popular demand could not be completely ignored. More schools were built. By 1909 about 10,000 students were in public schools; by 1913 the number of students had reached 46,000.[21] The schooling the French provided was closely controlled and was designed to give the Vietnamese the kind of education in Western values that was in keeping with French desires. Typical of this period were the technical institutions which were established. These institutions produced a number of low- and middle-level technical agents, trained in French and quốc ngữ. The French also began to sponsor a number of publications--weeklies, monthlies, and dailies--to defend or heap praises upon their *mission civilisatrice*, to counteract the impact of revolutionary, anti-French booklets, appeals, and tracts written by Phan Bội Châu, Phan Châu Trinh, and others.

PART III

On April 26, 1913, a member of the Association for the Restoration of Vietnam, under Phan Bội Châu threw a bomb at Hanoi Hotel in Hanoi, killing two French majors and wounding eleven other persons. In the middle of the next month, on May 15, 1913, *Đông Dương Tạp Chí* (Indochina Weekly) began publication. Its founder was a Frenchman named Schneider. The

editorial staff consisted of Nguyễn Văn Vĩnh, the
editor, four graduates of the School of Interpreters,
Phạm Quỳnh, Trần Trọng Kim, Nguyễn Văn Tố, and Phạm
Duy Tốn, and two Confucian scholars, Phan Kế Bính and
Nguyễn Đỗ Mục. All these persons became scholarly
men of letters and offered important contributions
to the literature in quốc ngữ.

In the first issue of the *Đông Dương Tạp Chí*
Schneider wrote, "Our weekly is published in a hurry
due to the terrorist act [the bombing of Hanoi
Hotel]. . . ."[22] and he concluded: ". . . together
we must use literature, knowledge, the benefits of
civilization to silence the rebellious words. We
ought to prevent the firecrackers of the rebels from
exploding, from exploding a sound against civilization."[23] The purpose of the French authorities was
clear. They wanted to use the *Đông Dương Tạp Chí*
for propaganda, to make the situation less tense,
to defend their colonial rule, to disseminate French
culture, and to discredit revolutionary writings and
activities.

But the editor, Nguyễn Văn Vĩnh, and his staff
also had the objectives of disseminating Western
knowledge in general, of popularizing quốc ngữ, and
of examining traditional values with a new spirit.
Nguyễn Văn Vĩnh (1882-1936) was a former interpreter
who had visited France in 1906-07 and later had be-

come the first Vietnamese to open a printing press
in Vietnam, in 1907. He was for complete modernization. He always wore European suits and rode a
motorcycle instead of using a horse-drawn carriage,
the fashionable means of transportation of the time.
In his weekly, Vinh launched an all-out attack
against the use of Chinese characters and the traditional prejudice of considering only poetic works
and parallel prose to be literary creations. He
wrote that Chinese characters were a barrier against
civilization; they exhausted students and obliged
them to spend many years and a great deal of money
in mastering them. When one finally became fluent
in characters, one already had creases on the fore-
head and a body bent from having spent one's life on
too-lofty things.[24] And in a foreword of a quốc ngữ
version of the *Truyện Kiều* he stated prophetically
that "in the future our country will progress or re-
gress, depending on quốc ngữ."[25] So he tried to
express himself, to write and translate in simple
quốc ngữ, in order to popularize it.

The *Đông Dương Tạp Chí* was published every
Thursday from 1913 to 1917. Each issue had about
thirty-two pages containing news of the country and
abroad, public affairs, government communiques, the
trade of France, essays on Buddhist, Confucian, and
Taoist concepts, poetry, and translations of Western

works on literature, philosophy, and science. But
readers of the time seemed to be most interested in
translations of novels from other countries--from
China and from Europe, especially France.

The two Confucian scholars on the staff of the
Đông Dương Tạp Chí used their knowledge of Chinese to
translate many Chinese novels. Most of these translations were serialized in their weekly or some
other paper and later published in book form. Phan
Kế Bính translated into quốc ngữ, among other works,
the *Romance of the Three Kingdoms*, which delighted
Vietnamese of all walks of life and popularized the
three heroes, Li Pei, Kuan Vu, and Chang Fei, as
symbols of brotherhood, fidelity, and integrity.
The second scholar, Nguyễn Đỗ Mục, was the most
famous translator of Chinese works, especially
novels. He translated, for instance, the Chinese
love novels *Sông Phương Kỳ Duyên* and *Tái Sinh Duyên*,
which became very popular among Vietnamese women.
They sympathized with the heroines of the novels,
Chiêu Quân and Mạnh Lê Quân, who suffered persecution by treacherous mandarins.[26] Mục also loosely
translated the Chinese novel *Tây Sương Ký*, which was
serialized in the *Đông Dương Tạp Chí* in numbers 28-
31, and the historical account *Đông Chu Liệt Quốc*,
also serialized in the weekly and later published in
book form. So the Vietnamese reading public got to

know Chinese prose novels through translations. Mục
put the Chinese version of the French novel *Sans
Famille* by Hector Malot into quốc ngữ. In addition,
he translated many other Chinese novels of adventure
and fantasy till the 1930s. His prolific work made
his name almost synonymous with any translations of
a Chinese novel.

The dynamic editor of the weekly, Nguyễn Văn
Vĩnh, in addition to his writings and his transla-
tions of French philosophical works and plays, also
translated many French and Western novels, such as
Gil Blas de Santillane by Lesage, *Gulliver's Travels*
by Swift, the *Aventures de Télémaque* by Fénelon,
Les Trois Mousquetaires by Alexandre Dumas, *Manon
Lescaut* by Abbé Prévost, *La Peau de Chagrin* by
Honoré de Balzac, *Les Misérables* by Victor Hugo, and
even *Les Fables* by La Fontaine.

Most educated Vietnamese at the time had not
mastered French well enough to enjoy works in the
original French. But many of them did enjoy the
translations of these novels. Indeed, although the
traditional civil-service examinations were not
abolished until 1915 in Tongking and 1918 in Annam,
by 1910 there already had emerged a small Western-
oriented, French-trained middle class of clerks,
foremen, noncommissioned officers, nurses, account-
ants, technical agents in public works and agricul-

ture, and graduates of a few middle-level schools in medicine, engineering, and pedagogy, who knew little Chinese but could read some French and quốc ngữ.

Another practical factor which caused many people to study quốc ngữ and French was that these two languages were supplanting Chinese as the language of the administration at all levels. Requests, petitions, and administrative papers were more and more being written in quốc ngữ instead of Chinese or *chữ nôm*. To make a living inside or outside the administration, one increasingly had to know French or, at least, quốc ngữ. The learning of Chinese gradually came to be regarded as useless. The poet Tú Xương wrote ironically:

> The Chinese characters don't count for any-
>   thing;
> The doctor or licentiate in Chinese remains
>   idle.
> It would be better to study to become a
>   clerk;
> At night one drinks champagne, in the morn-
>   ing milk.[27]

Many of the new middle class read *Đông Dương Tạp Chí* or some other newspaper and books or booklets in quốc ngữ. The weekly did have an impact upon the society. Its influence appears to have been more literary than political, but its political purpose

must not be forgotten. It contained a number of
articles heaping abuse upon Vietnamese patriots like
Phan Bội Châu, who was carrying on his anti-French
activities abroad. But, on the positive side,
through the writings and translations of Nguyễn Văn
Vĩnh and his collaborators in the magazine and elsewhere, the use of quốc ngữ for new literary genres
and to present new, Western ideas became apparent.
Quốc ngữ became popular, and through this medium the
Vietnamese reading public got to know Chinese and
French and other Western classical and contemporary
novels.

Another factor that contributed to the popularization of quốc ngữ and to the more widespread dissemination of novels in translation was the publication of additional newspapers. Before World War I
the *Nhật Báo Tỉnh* in quốc ngữ first saw the light of
day in Cochinchina in 1905; in Tongking in the same
year the *Đại Việt Tân Báo*, in Chinese and quốc ngữ
began publication, and later the *Đại Nam Đồng Văn
Nhật Báo*, or *Đông Cổ Tùng Báo*, also in Chinese and
quốc ngữ. These newspapers were sponsored or supported partly or entirely by the colonial authorities; they were mostly designed for the dissemination
of news. They contained government communiques,
speeches, and instructions from the administration.
Gradually they acquired more of a literary and

cultural content, with poems, essays, and translations of Chinese or French works. Furthermore, the
policy of the colonial administration was to make
efforts to guide public opinion in order to counteract the revolutionary writings of Vietnamese patriots. So more dailies were begun--the *Lục Tỉnh Tân
Văn* in 1910 in Saigon and the *Trung Bắc Tân Văn* in
1915 in Hanoi.

Indeed, the political situation around 1910
was no less tense than it had been during the preceding decade. The veteran guerrilla Hoàng Hoa Thám
was killed in 1913, and large populated areas in the
provinces of Bắc Ninh, Bắc Giang, Vĩnh Phúc, and
Phúc Yên were laid waste in a campaign of pacification. The Chinese revolution of 1911 and the writings of K'ang Yu-wei, Liang Ch'i-ch'ao, and others
continued to exert influence upon the educated class.
The French now and then relaxed their ruthless
policy of repression to calm the restlessness of the
dominated, to promote some unimportant reforms or
release some political prisoners. The reformist
Phan Châu Trinh was allowed to go to Paris in 1911;
he stayed there until 1925. He continued his anticolonial writings and activities and incidentally
taught a countryman, the future Nguyễn Ái Quốc,
alias Hồ Chí Minh, to develop film for a living.

The anticolonial cause was helped by the

lishing of publishing houses. In spite of strict
control and censorship, the newspapers were able to
let more people know about the events that were
happening in their country. Moreover, with the appearance of newspapers, magazines, and books, there
emerged in the large cities of Hanoi, Saigon, Hải-
Phòng, and, later, Huế a new kind of man of letters--
the newsman and writer, like Nguyễn Văn Vĩnh, the
editor of the *Đông Dương Tạp Chí*, who is considered
by some to be the father of Vietnamese journalism.

These new men of letters made a living with
their pens; they did not write for personal relaxa-
tion, as the Confucian scholars in the past had. In
producing for a living they had to cater to the
tastes of their customers, the reading public. Yet,
although they wrote to serve the masses, they felt
they had some mission, some duty to contribute to
social improvement. Most of them, in the first two
decades of the twentieth century, and even in the
1920s, were still Confucianized to a certain extent,
although they knew quốc ngữ and some French.

Typical of this transitional period among these
partly traditional, partly new men of letters was
the poet-writer Tản Đà Nguyễn Khắc Hiếu (1881-1939).
Failing in the mandarinal examinations, deceived in
his sentimental life, this writer to some extent tool

upon himself the mission of moral teaching, or re-
emphasizing the Confucian values of traditional Vietnam in the face of new ideas from the West. He had
some vague sympathy toward the people and used his
pen to call upon the masses to wake up. He casti-
gated corrupt officials, but he did not seem to have
any definite political attitude, nor was he anti-
French like Nguyễn Khuyến or Tú Xương. He was the
author of a prose work titled *The Small Dream*, published in 1917. It is a kind of diary. In it the
author dreams he is traveling to France, the United
States, South America, Brazil, back to Europe,
England, Norway, Sweden, to Moscow and Vladivostok,
from Japan to China, to Peking, through Szechwan,
from Tibet to India through the Himalayas, from
Pondicherry to Australia, Africa, Egypt, through the
Sahara, and then back to Vietnam, in eight years.[28]
It is a fantastic trip, even in imagination, for the
time. It shows the power of the imagination of the
author, and perhaps it also reflects the impact of
the "exodus to the East" and the Tongking School of
the Righteous Cause, in the longings of the Vietnamese for modernization, study abroad, and new
horizons. *The Small Dream* was commented on a great
deal by the writers of the time. It was strongly
criticized by Phạm Quỳnh, a former member of the
Đông Dương Tạp Chí staff and editor of the French-
213

sponsored *Nam Phong* (Southern Wind). As a cultural
henchman of the colonial authorities, Phạm Quỳnh
could not, as a North Vietnamese writer points out,
like the more-or-less progressive romanticism of
Tản Đà in the fantastic trip which he could only
consider characteristic of a "rebellious subject"
or a "whimsical person."[29] The French and their
collaborators apparently did not want the Vietnamese
to know countries other than France or to acquire
knowledge other than what they wanted them to have.

With the outbreak of the war between France and
Germany in 1914, the hopes of the Vietnamese people
for emancipation rose. A number of Vietnamese
revolutionaries got financial help from the Germans,
and Prince Cường Để even made a trip to Berlin. In
Vietnam a number of anti-French actions took place.
The revolutionaries Nguyễn Hải Thần and Hồ Tùng Mậu
attacked the French post of Tà Lùng at the Vietnam-
ese-Chinese frontier in 1915. The next year the
young king Duy Tân plotted with a number of patriots
in central Vietnam for an uprising against the French
and fled from the palace according to plan, but he
was captured, deposed, and exiled to the island of
Réunion. In the northern area Vietnamese soldiers
of the French army in the province of Thái Nguyên
revolted under a noncommissioned officer and occupied the provincial city for seven days. They were

inspired by Lương Ngọc Quyến, a Vietnamese graduate
of the Japanese Military Academy of Tokyo, who had
been arrested in Hongkong by British authorities,
turned over to the French, and jailed in Thái Nguyên.
The French government also recruited Vietnamese soldiers and workers--about a hundred thousand--for
their battlefields in Europe and imposed forced
loans on their colony. The situation in Indochina
at the time was full of tension and restlessness on
the part of the dominated.

PART IV

The French made renewed efforts to try to "sell"
their *mission civilisatrice* to the educated Vietnamese, who were at the head of most anti-French activities. They attempted to give to the still Confucianized men of letters some Western and French
education, some kind of cultural indoctrination, the
kind of knowledge the colonial government could
afford to let them have to satisfy their thirst for
Western learning. The *Đông Dương Tạp Chí*, under the
editorship of Nguyễn Văn Vĩnh, seemed to have outlived its usefulness and efficiency. Vĩnh and his
staff were more inclined to literary than to political
writing. It was necessary to propagandize for the

French cause in the war, to drum up more support from the colonies for the motherland. The director of the Political Service of the General Government of Indochina, Louis Marty, a very able and crafty agent who was fluent in both Chinese and quốc ngữ, instructed one of his native collaborators, Phạm Quỳnh, to publish a government-supported monthly named *Nam Phong*. Phạm Quỳnh (1892-1945), like Nguyễn Văn Vĩnh, Nguyễn Văn Tố, and many men of letters of the time, was self-taught. He was former librarian and had written for the *Đông Dương Tạp Chí*. According to his own account in the 1930s, he had proved his worth to the French general government by preparing a magazine in Chinese to be distributed in China to support the French cause against German propaganda.[30]

Nam Phong was published for seventeen years, from July 1917 to the end of 1934, in 210 issues. Each issue had three sections--in quốc ngữ, in French, and in Chinese--of about fifty pages each. The section in quốc ngữ is the most important, from the point of view of propagandizing for the French cause and disseminating knowledge. It contained essays on Western and Asian philosophy, culture, and science; it also contained literary commentary, research papers, editorials on current news, poetry, and serialized novels. The staff, in addition to

Phạm Quỳnh, consisted of noted writers and scholars, like Nguyễn Bá Học; Phạm Duy Tốn, who produced the first short stories in quoc ngu; Nguyễn Hữu Tiến; Nguyễn Trọng Thuật, the author of one of the first modern novels; the poet Đông Hồ; and the poetess Tương Phố.

Politically, Phạm Quỳnh tried to serve the cause of the colonialists. He wrote articles praising France and the French, the successive governors general and residents superior, and he lauded the puppet king Khải Định as the Meiji of Vietnam. The foreword of the first issue stated that the purpose of the publication was to present the *mission civilisatrice* of the government, to produce articles in quốc ngữ, Chinese, and French, to develop culture, to preserve morality among the Annamite people, to propagate Western--especially French--science and learning, to defend the soul and national spirit of Vietnam, and at the same time to protect the interests of French and Vietnamese citizens in the economic field.[31] Phạm Quỳnh heaped praises upon the humanism of France, upon French literature, philosophy, history, and religion, and French colonization. He wrote, "France took the colonies to protect backward people, to defend their interests, to educate them, to guide them to civilization."[32] And he concluded that such a way of taking colonies was

not an unvirtuous thing, but a righteous one.[33] It
is not surprising that in the 1930s Phạm Quỳnh made
the political jump from Hanoi to become the Minister
of the Interior of the puppet court at Huế, where
he remained until the end of the French domination
in March 1945. It is not hard to understand, either,
why the Việt Minh had him shot in the autumn of 1945.

Culturally, however, Phạm Quỳnh and *Nam Phong*
offered a great contribution to the popularization
of quốc ngữ, to the development of the various
modern literary genres in the literature in quốc ngữ,
and to the dissemination of knowledge, in general.
It is possible to learn much about the religions,
literatures, and cultures of China, Japan, and
France, about Vietnamese poetry from the Lý (1010-
1225) and Trần (1225-1400) dynasties to the present,
about the history of Vietnam and Vietnamese heroes,
about the social and political problems of East and
West, and about the theories of Greek and Latin
scholars, if one goes over the issues of *Nam Phong*.
In this magazine quốc ngữ was used for all kinds of
subjects, and it reached a high degree of maturity
in its expression. *Nam Phong* had a particularly
large number of articles on Western (especially
French) culture and literature, about Xavier de
Maistre, Paul Bourget, Pascal, Descartes, Baude-
laire, Guy de Maupassant, Voltaire, Lamartine, and

Chateaubriand, for example.

At first it seemed that Phạm Quỳnh wanted to propagate Western knowledge for the advancement of the people and country. But, in fact, he did not present the best of French culture, such as the most progressive ideas of self-determination and democracy in the French tradition of 1789. Instead, he chose conservative, monarchist writers like Xavier de Maistre and Paul Bourget or romantic poets like Lamartine and Chateaubriand. He also pretended to defend the soul, the cultural heritage of the Vietnamese, but in fact he reemphasized the Confucian values of loyalty to the monarch, of obedience, and of piety in the feudal sense, as he heaped praises upon *Truyện Kiều* in order to serve the colonial regime and the collaborationist administration. The people longed for Western knowledge, modernization. Since it was not proper or possible to eradicate these longings, the French and Phạm Quỳnh gave only the kind of knowledge they wanted their readers to have for a kind of progress at a slow pace, to divert them from the lingering impact of the "exodus to the East," of the Tongking School of the Righteous Cause, and of the revolutionary writings of Phan Bội Châu and Phan Châu Trinh, among others. Phạm Quỳnh did not present any plan for the application of Western values to the country. His purpose was seemingly to impart some uncoordinated, unsystematized knowledge of French literature and culture to his people. This was probably the reason why he so strongly criticized *The Small Dream* by Tản Đà Nguyễn Khắc Hiếu, which in its imaginary trip takes readers to many countries to see many new horizons besides the "motherland" France.

In 1921 Phạm Quỳnh did produce in *Nam Phong* an important article titled "Study on the Novel."[34] It is an essay on the technique of writing a novel following French literary procedures. He starts by telling of the growing number of those who read novels and characterizes those who attempt to create them:

> During the past few years, in our country, the number of those who write novels and who read them increases considerably. No beginning is perfect. Not only don't we have real writers but we also lack intelligent and enlightened readers, since the Vietnamese novel has no precise techniques. It appears to me to be the right time to define the novel and the Western technique of producing it.[35]

Phạm Quỳnh divides his study in four parts. In the first part he summarizes first the history of the novel in China and France and shows its impact upon society. He then states that the novel is an account in prose to describe the behavior of human beings,

220

the customs and habits of different societies, or to
relate extraordinary facts to attract readers. In
the second part, which is the most important, he
treats the structure of the French novel, which he
says can be summarized by the word *creation*--creation
of settings, situations, and characters. So a
novelist is a creator:

> The art of the novel is to invent an unreal
> story which is, however, based on real
> facts. So the reader, though he knows the
> story untrue, cannot prevent himself from
> believing it, since the characters would
> not act otherwise if they were real.[36]

He then examines the two usual ways of conceiving
action and characters: in one, the situation makes
the hero; in the other, the hero makes the situation. Phạm Quỳnh expresses his preference for the
first, since for him the characters in a novel are
not necessarily supermen, but ordinary men. He also
quotes the French critic Brunetière, who believes
that the art of the novel is to show that man in
spite of his claims is always at the disposition of
the situation he has to face and reacts accordingly.
Phạm Quỳnh insists on the creation of a real, or
nearly real, setting and shows that the French reflect the local characteristics of places and times
scrupulously. He also emphasizes that the French

novelist develops the action of the novel with
events, circumstances, trials, or episodes to pro-
voke the curiosity and interest of the reader, instead of announcing the outcome of the story before
even narrating it, as Chinese and Vietnamese novelists do.

As for the creation of characters, he points
out the difference between Western and Eastern ways.
For him, characters in novels of the East are only
symbols, concepts dressed up in human clothes, or
puppets pulled by the author; on the contrary, the
novelist in the West bases his hero on his observation. He shows that the hero of the French novel is
a live person, who talks and acts under our eyes and
evokes our responses. He suggests that Vietnamese
novelists pay more attention to the description of
the psychology of their characters. Phạm Quỳnh does
not seem to like romantic works but prefers the
classical portrayal of the human being, in general,
regardless of time and place.

In the third part of his study Phạm Quỳnh deals
with the form of the novel. The narration of Chinese and Vietnamese novels follows a chronological
order, whereas the French style is swift, varied, and
living, and the narrative varied by descriptions of
landscapes, psychological portraits, and dialogue.

In the fourth part he studies separately the

techniques appropriate to different kinds of novels,
such as the novel on passions, the novel of customs,
and the novel of adventure. In comparing the French
and the Vietnamese novel, he points out that, while
the Vietnamese novelist gives a secondary role to
love, his French counterpart in the contemporary
period makes love the prime mover of the account.

This study of the novel by Phạm Quỳnh is obviously biased in favor of the French novel. But it
was the first, or one of the first, theoretical
essays on this literary genre in quốc ngữ. It gives
information on the French novel, its meaning, structure, and technique, for the people of the transitional period in the 1920s, who were not yet well
versed in French and Western literary techniques.
It was indeed a useful contribution to the development of the modern novel in quốc ngữ. This study
was republished in book form in 1929.[37]

Phạm Quỳnh and his staff were very able writers.
Nam Phong was widely read, and its circulation
expanded greatly, thanks to the support of the administration, which "advised" hamlets, villages,
and districts to buy it. With the appearance of
Nam Phong, *Đông Dương Tạp Chí* faded away; and other
magazines which started later, such as *Đại Việt Tạp
Chí* in 1918, *Học Báo* in 1919, *Hữu Thanh* in 1931,
Phụ Nữ Tân Văn in 1929, the *Literary Magazine* in

1931, the *Movies Magazine* in 1932, and *Popular
Science* in 1934, did not have the large audience and
influence which *Nam Phong* had.

In this monthly, readers enjoyed, besides
articles on literary, social, and political subjects,
a number of translations or adaptations from Chinese
novels, such as *Chiếc Bóng Song The, Hoa Đào Trước
Gió, Thuyền Tình Bể Ái,* and *Văn Lan Nhật Ký.* All
these are very romantic love stories, having almost
the same kind of plot: love blooms between two
worthy young people, but because of obstacles they
have to part, heartbroken; sometimes the hero or
heroine dies of despair or seeks consolation in
religion or forgetfulness. In that period it was the
vogue to read and appreciate these sad love stories,
and many readers probably tried to see themselves in
the characters.

Nam Phong also printed many poems, especially
sad, romantic, gloomy ones which moved people or
made them shed tears. One, "Autumn Tears" by the
poetess Tương Phố Đỗ Thị Đam, is typical. This is a
half-prose, half-poetic work; the poetic parts are
like sobs, moans of sadness, since it is a wife weeping for her dead husband. The prose passages are
regrets, lamentations, sorrows:

Darling! I am lonely in my room. When-
ever I remember you, I stop sewing; folding
the material, I look out to the horizon,
remembering the roads, the walks by which
we went out and returned home, you and me;
hundreds and thousands of remembrances now
seem to take me back to the past while the
tide in my heart is also full of the waves
of tears. . . .38

Not to be surpassed by Tương Phố in this weeping and

moaning, a poet of the *Nam Phong* staff, Đông Hồ Lâm

Văn Phác, also cried for his wife in the "Diary of

Tears for Linh Phượng," which is as sad, gloomy, and

pathetic as "Autumn Tears." At the time, pathetic

and unfortunate love stories and sad poetry caught

the minds and imaginations of many Vietnamese, and

Phạm Quỳnh and *Nam Phong* fostered this trend of

personal, romantic sadness among the educated Viet-

namese.

In the same decade of the 1920s, however, many

literary genres from the West, such as the essay,

the editorial, the book review, and the news report,

first saw the light of day, or were developed, in

Nam Phong and other publications. The first modern

play in quốc ngữ, for instance, *The Cup of Poison* by

Vũ Đình Long, was published in *Hữu Thanh* magazine in

August 1921. Research papers in many fields of

philosophy, Confucianism, politics, society, law,

and the Vietnamese language were written in quốc ngữ.

To mention just a few, there were the works on

225

Confucianism and the history of Vietnam by the famous scholar Trần Trọng Kim and on proverbs and folk songs by Nguyễn Văn Ngọc and Phạm Quỳnh.

The success of the translations and adaptations of Chinese and French novels with the reading public, the growing number of magazines and dailies, the ability of quốc ngữ to express all ideas and sentiments, and the prevalence of prose over poetic forms in works in quốc ngữ encouraged writers to try their hands at writing original short stories and novels. The pioneer in this literary genre was a teacher named Nguyễn Bá Học (1857-1921), who published several short stories in *Nam Phong*. One of his works, "A Family Story," is about an old woman and her two sons: the elder studies Chinese and loses his opportunity in life with the coming of the French; the younger attends the new schools and gets a good job, but he adopts new, corrupt ways of life and causes a conflict in the family.[39] "The Story of Village Chief Cham" is the account of a simple notable in a village who has served his countrymen so well that he is remembered--worshiped--after his death.[40] "The Courage to Make Oneself Rich" relates the boldness of a bankrupt businessman who disguises himself as a worker, marries a poor girl, lives strictly, and succeeds in remaking his fortune.[41] "A Buddhist Monk's Story" is the pathetic account of an orphan boy who is raised and educated by a good woman and given her daughter in marriage.[42] He gets a good job as a government employee, but he grows dissipated; he becomes infatuated with a prostitute and tortures his wife to death to get her money. In the end he becomes a Buddhist monk to repent his misdeeds. "Miss Chiêu Nhị"[43] and "The Nuptial Night"[44] are two other moving stories. Miss Chiêu Nhị comes from a rich family, but she throws her money away and ends up as a beggar. In "The Nuptial Night" the husband notices that his wife is missing two fingers. Chinese foremen had annoyed her and made her fall into a machine that crushed the fingers. "A Dream" is the dream of a poor man who believes he has won a lottery prize and is enjoying a good life, until his wife wakes him up and asks him to sell his last shirt for rice.[45] "Adventures" is the account of a bad young man who seeks repentance by running after difficulties to start a new life.[46]

Through the short stories of Nguyễn Bá Học is reflected the transformation of Vietnamese society at the beginning of this century under the French. The author must have witnessed many changes, good and bad, pathetic and ironical, moral and immoral. His characters are usually members of traditional families who adopt new, Western ways of life and become corrupt, like the young son in "A Family Story" and the rich girl in "Miss Chiêu Nhị." The first glimpses of commercial, industrial activities, and of the Chinese comprador system are seen in "The Courage to Make Oneself Rich" and "The Nuptial Night." The author draws on his own observations as a resident for many years in the city of Nam Định, with its rice export and its spinning mill built by the French, the first in Vietnam.

Furthermore, it appears that Nguyễn Bá Học, like the Confucian scholars of his time, realized that Western civilization, based on industry and trade, could make the country prosperous. But, like them, he deplored the emphasis on a material life, which was destroying the traditional desire of the Vietnamese for a moral life and simple and strict living. Indeed, with the rights, duties, and privileges of the individual, the French also brought modern conveniences, material ways of life, and new pleasures, which tempted the Vietnamese youth. The new political system and education transformed the simple, poor student of yesteryear into a well-paid government employee who drank "milk in the morning and champagne at night." They also gave birth to luxurious restaurants, hotels, gambling houses, and brothels, which caused the degradation of many youths, as depicted in "A Buddhist Monk's Story," and by the younger son in "A Family Story," who gets the new education and causes a family conflict by leaving his mother, which would have been unthinkable in traditional Vietnam.

However, it is clear that the author, like most Confucian scholars of his time, is not against the material civilization of the West. To them, it is proper to make oneself rich and the country prosperous, but one should avoid the temptations of wealth. Miss Chiêu Nhị becomes a beggar because she wastes her money and, more seriously, because she wasted her time in her youth and did not learn any profession. Western education is still praised in "A Family Story," in spite of the improper behavior of the younger son. It is bad that Chinese foremen treat Vietnamese workers badly, for example, causing the woman in "The Nuptial Night" to lose two of her fingers, but this does not mean that one should be against industry and commerce, which develop the country; the lesson to be learned is that one should not let oneself be exploited.

The short story took another step forward with Phạm Duy Tốn (1883-1924). A graduate of the School of Interpreters, Phạm Duy Tốn resigned from government service to write and engage in commerce. His style was more modern than Nguyễn Bá Học's. He wrote in a simpler way and is easier to understand.

229

His best stories, such as "It Does Not Matter Whether They Live or Die"[47] and "Don Juan,"[48] were also published in *Nam Phong*. For the first time it appeared that prose writing in quốc ngữ had rid itself of Chinese influence by discarding such forms as the use of parallel phrases. The short stories of Phạm Duy Tốn are descriptive and realistic. In "It Does Not Matter Whether They Live or Die" one can see the sufferings of the peasants who are strengthening the dam against the rising floodwaters, while the "father and mother" of the people--that is, the mandarin in charge--is gambling in the village hall. Even after he is informed of the breakup of the dam, the mandarin still keeps on playing, not caring about the calamity. "Don Juan" is the portrayal of a scoundrel who fools a rich, honest girl and runs off with her money. Phạm Duy Tốn, while generally realistic in his stories, sometimes reflects the old style by inserting his comments in his description and moralizing now and then. But his works mark quite a progress toward the modern prose novel in the Western model. Phạm Duy Tốn is considered by some to be the pioneer in the writing of realistic short stories; his descriptions of corrupt mandarins under alien rule, for example, are considered to be accurate portrayals. By others he is seen as the symbol of emancipation from Chinese influence in modern Vietnamese quốc ngữ prose.

PART V

By the 1920s quốc ngữ had indeed superseded Chinese
characters and chữ nôm. Even French was taught in
schools through the medium of quốc ngữ. Quốc ngữ
had become the written language of Vietnamese in all
walks of life--peasants and scholars, educated men
and common people. All literary works were produced
in quốc ngữ; writers no longer produced in two
languages, one for the educated and one for the common people, as in the past. The unity of language
and literary production for the whole country and
the whole people was realized.

Furthermore, except for a small number of French
henchmen, members of the Vietnamese educated class,
whether former Confucian scholars or newly Western-
trained, were not in ruling positions. They were in
the same lot as the common mass, dominated by aliens.
Their education made them more aware of their personal predicament and that of their country. It was
members of this small minority of educated persons
who produced literary works, who spearheaded the
various movements of cultural, social, and political
protest and the resistance against the colonial

administration. They did so under different banners
and ideologies. But they knew that by themselves,
without the support of the masses, they could not do
much. So they paid much attention to the common
people--the peasants, artisans, and workers, the
poor, the exploited--to wake them up, to arouse them
to throw off the foreign yoke. In this way the common man received a fairer representation in literary
production in quốc ngữ than he had had in the past
literature in Chinese or chữ nôm. New ideas from
the West about democracy and popular rights also
contributed to this trend.

In addition, because of the ease of learning
quốc ngữ--the writing system could be mastered in
from three months to a year--more and more people
became literate. The French, like it or not, had to
open new schools, although the total enrollment was
not large. By 1924 about 62,000 male and 10,000
female students were attending schools in French
Indochina.[49] More newspapers were published; Central
Vietnam (Annam) acquired its first daily in 1927.
The reading audience grew larger and larger. Newspapers and periodicals at first printed translations
and adaptations of Chinese and French novels, which
were readily enjoyed, but readers gradually seemed
to demand more reading matter about their own environment and Vietnamese society. After the short stories

232

by Nguyễn Bá Học and Phạm Duy Tốn, the literary
stage was set for the modern novel, which made its
appearance in 1925 in Tongking, ten years after the
abolition of the traditional examinations in that
part of the country.

NOTES

[1]Nguyen Nhuoc Thi, *Hanh Thuc Ca* (Saigon, 1950), p. 38.

[2]Thanh Lang, *Bieu Nhat Lam Van Hoc Can Dai* (Saigon, 1958), p. 178.

[3]Le Thanh Khoi, *Le Vietnam: Histoire et Civilisation* (Paris, 1955), pp. 219-92).

[4]Thanh Lang, *Bieu Nhat*, p. 50.

[5]Ibid., pp. 50-54.

[6]Ibid., p. 75.

[7]Huynh Tinh Cua, *Chuyen Giai Buon* (Saigon, 1960).

[8]Nghiem Toan, *Vietnam Van Hoc Su* (Saigon, 1949), p. 141.

[9]Ibid.

[10]Truong Vinh Ky, *Chuyen Doi Xua* (Saigon, 1962).

[11]Pham The Ngu, *Vietnam Van Hoc Su 1862-1945* (Saigon, 1965), pp. 1-2.

[12]Ibid.

[13]J. L. de Lanessan, *La Colonisation Française en Indochina* (Paris, 1895), p. 30.

[14]Dan Thai Mai, *Van Tho Cach Mang Vietnam* (Hanoi, 1961), p. 40.

[15]Ibid., pp. 266-75.

[16]Ibid., pp. 24-25.

[17]Phuong Huu, *Phong Trao Dai Dong Du* (Saigon, 1951), pp. 12-13.

[18]Dang Thai Mai, *Van Tho Cach Mang*, pp. 48-50.

[19]Nguyen Hien Le, *Dong Kinh Nghia Thuc* (Saigon, 1956).

[20]Dang Thai Mai, *Van Tho Cach Mang*, p. 60.

[21]Jean Chesneaux, *Contributions à l'Histoire de la Nation Vietnamienne* (Paris, 1955), p. 196.

[22]*Dong Duong Tap Chi*, May 15, 1913.

[23]Ibid.

[24]In *Dang Co Tung Bao*, as quoted in Thanh Lang, *Bieu Nhat*, p. 178.

[25]Nhat Tam, *Nguyen Van Vinh* (Saigon, 1957), p. 10.

[26]Vu Ngoc Phan, *Nha Van Hien Dai*, (Hanoi, 1951) 1:67-68.

[27]Vien Van Hoc, *So Thao Lich Su Van Hoc Vietnam* (Hanoi, 1964), p. 232.

[28]Tam Duong, *Tan Dao Khoi Mau Thuan Lon* (Hanoi, 1964), p. 263.

[29]Ibid., p. 14.

[30]Interview of Pham Quynh by Dao Hung in *Phu Nu Nu Tan Van*, June 18, 1931.

[31]*Nam Phong*, 1(July 1917).

[32]Ibid.

[33]Ibid.

[34]Pham Quynh, "Ban Ve Tieu Thuyet," *Nam Phong*, 43(January 1921):1-16.

[35]Ibid., p. 4.

[36]Ibid., p. 8.

[37]Pham Quynh, *Khao Ve Tieu Thuyet* (Hanoi, 1929).

[38]Tuong Pho, "Giot Le Thu," *Nam Phong* 131(July 1928):15.

[39]"Cau Chuyen Gia Tinh," *Nam Phong* 10(April 1918).

[40]"Chuyen Ong Ly Cham," *Nam Phong* 13(July 1918).

[41]"Co Gan Lam Giau," *Nam Phong* 23(May 1919).

[42]"Chuyen Mot Nha Su," *Nam Phong* 26(August 1919).

[43]"Co Chieu Nhi," *Nam Phong* 43(January 1921).

[44]"Dem Tan Hon," *Nam Phong* 46(April 1921).

[45]"Giac Mo," *Nam Phong* 49(July 1921).

[46]"Du Sinh Lich Hiem Ky," *Nam Phong* 35(May 1920).

[47]"Song Chet Mac Bay," *Nam Phong* 18(December 1918).

[48]"Con Nguoi So Khanh," *Nam Phong* 20(February 1919).

[49]Chesneaux, *Contributions à l'Histoire*, p. 196.

JAPAN AND THE DISRUPTION OF THE
VIETNAMESE NATIONALIST MOVEMENT

By Trương Bửu Lâm

In the modern history of Southeast Asia, the years of
World War II have usually been referred to as the
Japanese interregnum. The designation implies that
colonial administrations, during these years, suffered no more than a "pause" in the control they
exercised over colonies, a control they quickly recaptured after the war. But an examination of events
in Southeast Asia after the war would seem to in-
validate the term *interregnum*. The French never
reestablished sovereign authority over their former
possessions in Indochina. The Dutch returned to
Indonesia, only to find opposition from an Indonesian government which had proclaimed the archipela-
go's independence two days after the capitulation of
the Japanese. The British confronted negotiations
on the independence of Burma, even as insurgency
shook Malaya, an insurgency which subsided only
after autonomy had been promised to the peninsula.
In the Philippines in 1946 an independent republic
was proclaimed. The Japanese period, therefore,
more or less abruptly ushered in the end of the old

237

Western dominance over Southeast Asia. The word
interregnum, then, would be meaningful only if it
were to mean that the period saw Southeast Asia's
transition from political dependence to political
independence.[1] Although Japan's presence in Southeast Asia was short-lived, it exerted an influence
on the area still to be reckoned with today.

Needless to say, Japan's influence varied greatly from country to country. There did not exist a
single, comprehensive Japanese blueprint for the
entire area. Japanese documents of the years 1940
and 1941 show clearly that, apart from Japan's
ultimate goal of creating the Co-prosperity Sphere,
an economically self-sufficient sphere under the
control of Japan, Tokyo premeditated few other
political designs for any of the countries that the
imperial army would liberate from colonial rule. To
adapt policy to circumstances, whatever there might
be, seems to have been the main consideration of the
Japanese cabinet.[2] It was local exigencies, more
than anything else, that led the Japanese army to
take over from colonial authorities the administration of all Southeast Asian countries, all except
French Indochina.[3] The Japanese undertook either to
rule Southeast Asian countries themselves--as in
Malaya and Singapore--or at least partially to trans-
fer that rule to indigenous regimes composed of

238

persons favorable to their goal--as in the Philippines, Indonesia, and Burma. Vietnam, in my view,
represents a notable exception to the pattern.
Vietnam, or more precisely French Indochina, remained
under French rule almost throughout the duration of
World War II. I will try to show how the French,
the Japanese, and the forces that opposed them inter-
acted during the troubled years of the world conflict and what effects that interaction had on the
Vietnamese nationalist movement.

Thanks to the Vichy regime's collaboration with
Germany in Europe, the French administration in
Indochina managed to live alongside the Japanese for
five years. The presence in France after June 1940
of a government linked to Germany provided Japan
with a golden chance to dictate terms concerning her
presence in Indochina. In other countries, Japan
encountered hostility from both colonial administration and metropolitan governments. In Indochina
colonial authorities remained under the control, however loose, of Vichy. They consequently collaborated
with Japan, on the latter's terms. After the Japanese arrived, it was still French civil servants who
assured administrative continuity in the region, and
it was the French army and police who undertook to
maintain law and order. Thanks to this, Japan
economized on a large number of troops she would

otherwise have been obliged to station at routine
posts.

At first, Japan conceived of Indochina as part
of her South China theater of operations, to which
it was, indeed, related. Unloaded at the port of
Hảiphòng, military materials were being channeled
through Tongking and by the Yunnan railroad to the
Chinese national army. Already, on 20 June, 1940,
under pressure from the Japanese government, General
Catroux, the governor general of Indochina, had to
close the Indochinese frontier to all military ship-
ments to China and to agree to the posting in Hanoi
of a Japanese military mission, whose duty it was to
"supervise all materials destined for China."[4] It
must not be supposed, however, that Vichy welcomed
these concessions to Japan. For his part in them,
Catroux was replaced by Vichy with Admiral Jean
Decoux, believed to be more amenable to metropolitan
views. At the same time, P. Baudouin, the Vichy
Minister of Foreign Affairs, made it clear to the
Japanese ambassador to France, Sawada, that Vichy
meant to remain the master of Indochina's destiny
and that any affairs relating to Indochina should be
discussed with Vichy and not with the colonial
authorities on the spot in Indochina.[5] The position
was agreed to by Tokyo, and henceforth all negotiations were conducted through the French embassy in

Tokyo and the Japanese mission in Paris.

The French government in Vichy and the French colonial administration in Hanoi were both aware of the Japanese need for access to Indochina and of the impossibility of denying it to her. For a while, Vichy had hoped that the United States and Germany would restrain Tokyo's ambitions. But, upon finding the United States noncommittal and Germany unable to sway Japan,[6] Vichy yielded to Tokyo's demands. On August 30, 1940, a political accord was signed in Tokyo, in which the Japanese government pledged to recognize French sovereignty in Indochina and to respect French territorial integrity in that part of the world, in return for which principles France agreed to acknowledge Japan's preeminence in the Far East.[7] To translate these abstract notions into concrete realities, a military protocol was to be negotiated between the governor general of Indochina and General Nishihara, chief of the Japanese military mission in Hanoi. Governor General Decoux advocated a firmer opposition to Japanese demands and used several tactics to delay the signing of the protocol. A Japanese ultimatum, coupled with a threat to support Siamese claims to Cambodia and Laos, finally forced the Indochinese administration to sign the military protocol on

September 20, 1940. In it, Japan was given the use
of three airports in North Vietnam and the right to
station 6,000 troops in the area; she was not to send
more than 25,000 troops at any one time across Indochina, and she was to use the port of Håiphòng when
transporting troops to or from South China.[8]

These accords notwithstanding, on September 22,
1940, the Japanese army of Canton crossed over into
Vietnam and attacked and routed several French
garrisons stationed in the province of Langsơn.
Perhaps the incident resulted from a lack of co-
ordination between the Canton army, the Japanese
military mission in Hanoi, and the cabinet in Tokyo.
In my judgment, however, the Japanese simply wished
both to test French strength and to display Japanese
power. The test proved conclusive: the French in
Indochina showed themselves incapable of putting up
any significant resistance to the Japanese. From
then on, French administrators and Japanese occu-
piers, clearly realizing their respective strengths,
both renounced military contest, and instead each
did his utmost to win the support of the Indochinese
population.

The French administrators, under Admiral Decoux,
found themselves in the best of times. All relations
with the mother country being practically cut off,
Decoux governed the colony pretty much as he pleased.

242

As for the Japanese, throughout the war years until
1945, they made no attempt to replace the French in
their daily administration of Indochina. Japanese
troops stationed in Indochina were few in number and
were generally confined to strategic positions. The
French governor general could therefore, unhindered,
devote his energy to the realization of the chief
goal of his administration, which was to maintain,
as best he could, twenty-five million Indochinese
under French control.[9] He pursued this goal in many
ways. One was to take swift and harsh measures
against all Vietnamese attempts at rebellion. The
French could not resist Japan, but they were more
than equipped to pacify local unrest. In this, they
encountered no obstacle from the Japanese. In the
early days of their occupation of Indochina, the
Japanese were not prepared to support the Vietnamese
drive for independence from France. The aftermath
of the Lạng-sơn incident and events in southern Vietnam in 1940 proved the point beyond doubt. Trần
Trung Lập, the leader of the Vietnam Restoration
League (Việt-Nam Phục Quốc Đồng Minh Hội), an anti-
French organization, when he saw Japan's easy victory
in Lạng-sơn on September 22, 1940, decided to take
advantage of the situation and launch his own units
against the same battered French garrisons. When
the Mikado ordered his troops to cease fire on

243

September 25, the Vietnamese rebellion continued to
spread to the entire province of Lạngsơn. It was
not put down until the end of December, after the
French had captured and executed Trần Trung Lập.
The Japanese, in the meanwhile, had calmly watched
the repression. It has been said that Trần Trung
Lập's uprising was "carefully coordinated" with the
Japanese attack on Lạngsơn and that his units were
armed through the "generosity of the Japanese."[10]
Such an interpretation would appear plausible at
first, considering the long association between
Japan and the Vietnam Restoration League. Among the
league's founders had been Phan Bội Châu and Prince
Cường Để, long-time sojourners in Japan. But on
closer examination it would appear unlikely that
Japanese and Vietnamese attacks comprised a joint
operation. First of all, the Canton army would hardly have given arms to the Vietnamese without explicit
orders from Tokyo. And yet it was clearly not the
policy of the Japanese government in those early
years to aid Vietnamese nationalists. And would
Tokyo have decided to launch the Phục Quốc on
September 22, only to call a cease-fire three days
later and then passively watch its suppression in
the ensuing months? Rather, the simultaneity of the
Japanese attack and the Phục Quốc uprising should,
in my view, be seen simply as an attempt by the Phục

Quốc to capitalize on French weakness in order to seize power, at least in the province of Lạng-sơn. The sizable military equipment at their disposal-- 5,000 rifles, 20 automatic weapons, 25,000 rounds of ammunition, and 3,000 grenades--is not overly impressive when one considers the fact that the Phục Quốc had been active for years in that region.

In November of the same year (1940) the French faced yet another uprising, this time in southern Vietnam. Upon hearing of the Japanese entrance into northern Vietnam and of the threatened Siamese invasion of eastern Cambodia and southern Laos, the Communists staged a general insurrection throughout the South, but with particular force in the province of Mỹ-tho.[11] The plot had been known to the French security service, and when the rebellion actually flared up on November 22, it was easily crushed.[12] The repression was harsh,[13] and, here again--understandably this time because it concerned a Communist uprising--the Japanese did not intervene on behalf of the Vietnamese.

Another form of control employed by the French was rather milder. They tried, for example, to redress certain long-standing Vietnamese grievances. Ever since the 1920s, the matter of the differential in salaries paid to French and Indochinese civil servants had been bitterly resented. It had been a

colonial principle that the lowest-ranked representative of France in Indochina must receive a
salary superior to that of the highest Indochinese
official employed by the colonial administration.
In 1941 Decoux abolished this fine discrimination
and proclaimed instead the principle of equality in
salaries. Henceforth, French civil servants, in
addition to the pay granted their Vietnamese counter-
parts, would receive only a small allowance called
the indemnity of expatriation. Decoux also tried
to enhance the prestige of the mandarins in the
Vietnamese administration by raising their salaries
and by imparting a little splendor to their careers;
for example, he ordained that the results of the
mandarinal examinations be announced with pomp and
ceremony. Decoux righted yet another wrong. The
Indochinese people until then had been prevented
from occupying certain high positions in the civil
and technical services. During the war, because
replacements could not come from metropolitan
France, Decoux decided to open these positions to
the indigenous peoples. Consequently, the number of
Vietnamese in the middle and higher ranks of the
civil service doubled in the period from 1940 to
1945.[14] "In education, public works, customs and
public health, Vietnamese filled every position at
the chief of provincial department level. In the

postal service and the railroads, the French presence dwindled to a few dozen."[15] Some Vietnamese were even made provincial chiefs, the highest appointment possible at the local level in the general administration of the country. That had never happened before in the annals of Vietnamese colonial history.

Although representative institutions were bound to suffer in wartime, and, indeed, Admiral Decoux abolished all colonial councils, still he replaced them with the Federal Council of Indochina, to which he appointed more than twenty-five prominent Indochinese, all "chosen for their merit and their loyal sentiments towards France."[16] Finally, in order to give a large number of the Indochinese a feeling of superiority, of selectness, the French administration issued a luxurious publication titled *Souverains et Notabilités de l'Indochine*. The book contained pictures and biographical sketches of all Indochinese who, in one way or another, had distinguished themselves in the service of their respective countries and, for the most part, in their loyal collaboration with the French.[17]

The young, too, were held under control with various measures. In spite of the war, the University of Hanoi not only continued its activities but even expanded its enrollment.[18] At lower levels of education, many new schools were opened, and the number of students grew from 450,000 in 1939 to 700,000 in 1944.[19] The student bodies were closely watched and heavily indoctrinated. Sensing that nationalistic sentiments were making headway among the young, the French tried to channel them into acceptable outlets. Students were permitted, and even encouraged, to speak of independence, but only of an independence that allowed for association with France. Outside the schools and, in fact, throughout the length and breadth of Indochina, the commissioner of sports and youth, Maurice Ducoroy, mobilized the population in an ambitious, unprecedented, and highly propagandistic program of athletic competition and social action. Ducoroy organized everything imaginable to prevent the Japanese from, to quote his words, "gathering these Indochinese youths and inciting them against France."[20] He sponsored bicycle tours of Indochina modeled on the Tour of France, relays to carry Olympic-like flames from city to city, and tennis championships; and he founded hotel and farm schools. The Vichy regime's slogan "National Revolution" was applied to Indochina and the virtues of "Work, Family, and Fatherland" broadcast to all. The object behind this vast undertaking was to remind the Indochinese people that the French were still very much in control and to demonstrate to the Japanese

that the Indochinese still stood firmly behind their
French masters. And, as a matter of fact, while the
Indochinese elite understood perfectly well that the
French concessions represented a wartime stratagem
and not a fundamental shift in colonial policy, they
nevertheless gave the French their support as they
had been wont to, for they saw no new choice. Theirs
had been the careers of civil servants, French-
trained technicians and professionals, and although
they sincerely wished for the independence of their
country, they believed no less sincerely in coöperation with the colonial power.

With the elite neutralized by a generous policy
and with the young addicted to athletics and a safe
form of nationalism, the colonial administration
could concentrate its efforts on crushing those who
tried to oppose their administration in any effective
way.

What Japan's exact plans for Vietnam were is difficult to pinpoint. Notwithstanding the popular and
well-known slogan "Asia for the Asiatics," Japan
coöperated with the French administration in Indochina even after the entire Southeast Asian theatre
of operations had fallen to the Japanese army. In
fact, it can even be said that from 1940 until 1942
the Japanese chose outright to deal with the French

rather than the Vietnamese, because the former's experience in maintaining law and order in Indochina permitted the Japanese army to be deployed in other areas of Southeast Asia. But even after 1943, when Japanese occupational administrations elsewhere, in such areas as the Philippines, Burma, and Indonesia, had already yielded somewhat to local pressures for independence, Japan continued to preserve the French administration and to allow it to govern its Indochinese colony pretty much as before.[21] It is true that no Southeast Asian country achieved full political independence under the Japanese. Nevertheless, elsewhere in Southeast Asia colonial masters were removed and the local people were permitted to participate more fully in the administration of their own countries. In Indochina, however, the Japanese government appears to have followed quite closely the recommendations prepared in early 1942 by the Total War Research Institute, in that "the French were to be retained, subject to close scrutiny, and no independence movement would be permitted."[22] In view of the past relationships between Japan and Vietnamese anticolonial leaders, this position was most unexpected. In fact, one of these leaders, Prince Cường Để, was residing in Japan even as Japanese forces occupied Indochina. He had gone to Japan in 1905 at the prompting of Phan Bội Châu, one of Vietnam's most

250

prominent anti-French leaders, to enlist Japanese support for the nationalist cause. Although in 1908 and 1909, under French pressure, the Japanese government had expelled most Vietnamese residents from its territory, Vietnamese nationalists nevertheless continued to look on Japan as the champion of Asian nationalism. From the Japanese side, prominent Japanese, among them Prime Minister Inukai, himself, maintained regular contacts with Prince Cường Để and the remaining Vietnamese nationalists. In view of this long relationship between the Japanese and the Vietnamese nationalists, it seems most surprising that Japan appears neither to have expected, nor prepared for, a local pro-Japanese government.

For obvious ideological reasons, the Indochinese Communist party was unacceptable to Japan. Furthermore, as early as 1937, after the Japanese had invaded China, the Indochinese Communist party had sided with China in opposition to Japanese expansion.[23] In 1939 Hồ Chí Minh had advocated that the Indochinese Communist party in effect forgo its ideological exclusivity and form a democratic front with the national bourgeoisie, and even the progressive French, to resist Japanese fascism.[24]

Besides the Indochinese Communist party, however, there existed in Indochina a great number of political groups which might have been attracted

easily enough into a close relationship with Japan
and thus have effected a smooth transition from
French rule to Japanese-sponsored independence. Instead, the Japanese in Vietnam chose to encourage
the least likely elements in Vietnamese politics. In
addition to promoting a few relatively respectable
individuals in the Đại Việt party, the Japanese lent
wholehearted supported to the Cao-đài and the Hòa-
hảo, two politico-religious sects. The Cao-đài
religion was founded in 1926 in southern Vietnam by
a group of civil servants. Caodaism is characterized
by its ideological electicism and its concern with
the world of spirits. The highest divinity is the
Cao-đài (literally, Supreme Palace), and he is
represented by a single eye. Under him are a number
of coequal personalities, among them Jesus, Muham-
mad, Confucius, Lao-tse, the Buddha, and Victor Hugo.
Through various channels such as mediums and ritual
objects, the Cao-đài communicates his will to his
followers. Caodaism is organized into a church with
a pope at its head, who resides at his holy see in
Tây-ninh.[25] Caodaism made tremendous conversions
among the peasantry in southern Vietnam, and toward
the beginning of World War II the number of its adherents amounted to about half a million.[26] The
leaders of the Cao-đài religion had been contacted
by Japanese agents as early as the mid-1930s, and

252

from then on the Cao-đài gradually added an anti-
French element to their ideology. Although the
French administration recognized Caodaism as a legal
religion soon after its inception, still French
security services kept its activities under constant
scrutiny. From the moment the Japanese arrived, the
French sensed that the Cao-đài would cause trouble.
They therefore decided to close down their principal
temple in Tây-ninh in 1940. In 1941 they sent the
most prominent personalities of the Cao-đài hier-
archy, including Phạm Công Tắc, the pope, into exile.
The new committee formed to govern the sect, headed
by Trần Quang Vinh, openly sought and quickly received the protection of the Japanese. Thus started
a close collaboration in which the Cao-đài provided
the Japanese with the labor of more than 3,000 workers for their naval and road repairs, in return for
which the Japanese trained a Cao-đài militia of no
less than 20,000 men.[27] That same year--1941--the
French arrested Huỳnh Phú Sổ, the founder of the Hòa-
hảo, on the grounds that he had become insane. The
Japanese Kempeitai freed him, took him to Saigon,
and kept him there under its protection. This
action, alone, ensured the Japanese of the full support of the entire sect, which was very devoted to
its leader. Hòa-hảo is a modified form of Buddhism--
the Buddhism of peace and harmony, as its name im-

plies. The province of South Vietnam in which it originated, Long-xuyên, was famous for its magical and insurrectionary activities, and the personality of the founder, Huỳnh Phú Sổ, represented the province well. Huỳnh Phú Sổ was known as a highly sensitive man; furthermore, he was said to be endowed with the power of healing sicknesses and was thought to be invulnerable to weapons. The sect met with tremendous success in the region of its origin, and at the outbreak of World War II, hardly two years after its foundation, its adherents amounted to several hundred thousand.[28]

The Japanese thus received the collaboration of two very important groups. These groups, however, operated exclusively in southern Vietnam. Furthermore, because of the highly spiritualistic qualities of both sects, they enjoyed little political influence outside their respective congregations.

Aware of the shortcomings of the sects, the Japanese decided to support one other group, the Đại Việt. It is most difficult to learn anything definite about the Đại Việt because, in addition to the dark which usually surrounds political parties in colonial countries, this group functioned not quite as a party, but as a secret society or political fraternity. Moreover, under the general name of Đại Việt, there were lumped together a number of splinter

groups professing **various** tendencies, having in common only that (1) they traced their origins to organizations founded by Phan Bội Châu between 1905 and
1925 and (2) they admired Japan for executing the
most brilliant feat of modernization in Asian history. Another characteristic of these groups was that
they catered to the elite and not to the masses. To
this day, members of the Đại Việt pride themselves
that theirs is a party for the elite. Their political activities chiefly consisted of maneuvering their
members into positions of command in the power structure. The careful building of a party organization
did not further their particular interests, and they
quite neglected it. For this reason, the Đại Việt
has always lacked a strong concrete platform. Ulti-
mately, of course, the Đại Việt sought independence
for Vietnam. With this goal in mind, they collaborated with the Japanese in the hope that the day
would come when Japan would help them rid themselves
of the French. Given its nature, the Đại Việt lacked
a really important following. Needless to say, not
all Đại Việt groups collaborated with the Japanese in
Vietnam: a few of them were operating underground
against the French and the Japanese, while others
still worked in South China along with other political parties in the Alliance for the Independence of
Vietnam (Việt Minh).

The Cao-đài, the Hòa-hảo, the Đại Việt--these were the three main groups that the Japanese won over. The latter were not unaware of the lack of common purpose, let alone coördination, among their proteges. To remedy the situation, they summoned them to form the Alliance for the National Restoration of Vietnam. The figure around whom the new formation rallied was Cường Để. At the time, he was living in Japan, and the Japanese thought of taking him back to Vietnam to personify the spirit of the new alliance and also to attract the support of those monarchists who felt that the ruling dynasty had been too compromised by its close association with the colonial power. From 1943 on, Japanese propaganda positively prepared for his return. Several Vietnamese newspapers, apparently under orders from the Japanese, related in great detail the revolutionary career of Cường Để, as well as his prominent role in the nationalist cause.[29] Cường Để, as it turned out, never did return to his country.

On March 9, 1945, the Japanese, feeling threatened by the activities of the Free French in Indochina and prodded by their Vietnamese collaborators, staged a coup d'état against the French. They rounded up all French administrators and troops stationed in Indochina, disarmed them, and put them either under house arrest or into barracks under lock and key. Two days later, the Emperor of Vietnam Bảo Đại repudiated all treaties signed with France. A month later, on April 17, a government was formed under the premiership of Trần Trọng Kim, a well-known historian who had been suspected by the French of anticolonial activities. The Japanese had protected him during most of the war; they had arranged for him to go to Singapore and so escape an attempted arrest by the French security services.[30] Trần Trọng Kim's cabinet was surprisingly nonpartisan in its composition. The ministers were men distinguished in scholarship or in the professions. Only one or two would seem to have been directly involved with the Đại Việt party. The government was obviously one of technicians, not politicians, and as such could have appealed to a relatively large proportion of the Vietnamese people. The real power, nevertheless, remained in the hands of the Japanese. The Trần Trọng Kim government, for example, lacked a Defense Ministry, and, of course, it had no army. Furthermore, it exercised no control over the southern part of Vietnam, Cochinchina, which had been a colony of France and now remained under the direct administration of the Japanese military.

Two questions need to be raised here, if not answered. Why did the Japanese not take Cường Để back to Vietnam before 1945, and why did they

257

frustrate the unity of Vietnam by imposing a direct
rule over Cochinchina? I confess that I have not
found a satisfactory answer to the first question.
An explanation I have been given is that the Japanese
eventually decided that Cường Để was not equal to the
task of being chief of state. Another speculation
has it that the Japanese did not consider the situation ripe for him in 1943, and by 1945 their own
position had so deteriorated that they no longer
envisaged any serious undertaking in Vietnam. According to Mr. Masayuki Yokoyama, on the other hand,
if the Japanese did not take Cường Để back, it was
not because they did not want him, but simply because
of his advanced age and poor health.[31] Whatever the
exact reasons were for passing over Cường Để, the
Japanese finally chose to keep Bảo Đại as chief of
state, even though he had been closely associated
with the French colonial administration. Disorgan-
ized and pressed as they were for time, the Japanese
seem to have elected the simplest short-run solution: Bảo Đại was on the spot, and his administration, with Japanese help, could assure the continuity
and order required by circumstances. Nevertheless,
much more work needs to be done on this subject, in
which particular attention must be paid to the possibly conflicting roles played by the various branches of the Japanese government in backing different

Vietnamese candidates. One is left to wonder whether the course of Vietnamese history would have been appreciably altered had Cường Đế been brought back in 1943.

As for the Cochinchinese question, several explanations have been advanced, none of them quite satisfactory, either. Perhaps the most plausible reason for the Japanese action lies in the fact that Saigon lay at the center of their military operations in Indochina. It would seem that the city in fact had become the focus of their entire Southeast Asian push. It was to the military command in Saigon that the Japanese summoned Sukarno and other Indonesian leaders to discuss Indonesian independence. Although the Trần Trọng Kim government's authority in Annam and Tongking remained largely symbolic, the Japanese probably wished to avoid even this symbolic restraint on their activities in the crucial Cochinchina area. The official explanation given by the Japanese for their action was that Cambodia claimed Cochinchina for herself. Then, too, Cochinchina was the strong-hold of Japan's staunchest allies, the Cao-đài and the Hòa-hảo. As long as Japan retained control over Cochinchina, she could offer it, alternatively, to Cambodia and to the religious sects in return for their coöperation. As it turned out, on the eve of their capitulation the Japanese authorities in Saigon turned Cochinchina over to the Trần Trọng Kim government.

Meanwhile, the internal situation in Vietnam took a turn for the worse. The Trần Trọng Kim government, lacking any experience in political organization, relied exclusively on the civil services to implement its policy. These had been badly impaired by the removal of their French staff. The situation reached such a point that the Japanese were all but ready to summon the French employees back. It was only under very strong opposition from the Vietnamese government that they refrained from doing so. Furthermore, intense Allied bombing had reduced communication in the country to a bare minimum. The chaos in which the country found itself prompted political groups to intensify their activities, the greatest part of which were directed both against the Japanese and the Vietnamese governments. Among these groups, the Việt Minh figures prominently.

The Việt Minh organization is relatively well known and need not be discussed in detail here. It was a political coalition founded in South China in 1941 by several anti-French and, to a lesser degree, anti-Japanese groups. The pillar of the organization was the Indochinese Communist party. As an anti-Japanese organization, the Việt Minh received the full support of the Allies, among whom were the

260

Americans, the Free French, and the Chinese. In
spite of the harsh repression they encountered from
both the French and the Japanese, Việt Minh cadres
managed to maintain and propagate secret cells in
almost every city, village, and hamlet in Vietnam.[32]
This network enabled them to provide the Allies with
continuous and generally accurate information on
Japanese movements. Besides consolidating their own
strength, the Việt Minh also infiltrated all pro-
French and pro-Japanese organizations, particularly
the youth organizations, such as the Vanguard Youth,
which had been set up by the Japanese in Cochinchina
to back their own troops up directly.[33] Their
ground thus well laid, immediately upon hearing the
news of the Japanese surrender, the Việt Minh set out
in a sweeping campaign to wrest power from the Trần
Trọng Kim government. Launched on August 17, 1945,
their campaign came to a successful end ten days
later. By August 27, the entire territory of Vietnam
had fallen to Việt Minh control. Việt Minh commit-
tees were set up in all the provinces to administer
them. In the meanwhile, on August 23 in the imperial
city of Huế Emperor Bảo Đại abdicated, and the Trần
Trọng Kim government, which had already resigned on
August 18, transferred its power to a Việt Minh committee. On August 30, representatives of the Việt
Minh went to Huế to receive from the hands of Emperor

Bảo Đại the sword and the seal, symbols of power and
authority, at a formal ceremony of abdication. Three
days later, in Hanoi, Hồ Chí Minh proclaimed the
independence of Vietnam and the formation of a pro-
visional government for the Democratic Republic of
Vietnam. All political groups, at least for a
while, accepted the leadership of the Việt Minh, and
everywhere, it seemed, the word *independence* spread
and made a deep impression on the people.

This rather heady state of affairs did not last
long, however. Quick on the heels of the British
occupation troops, charged with disarming the Japanese in the southern part of Vietnam, appeared the
French, sent by de Gaulle's government and bent on
reestablishing colonial control over all of Indochina. In the northern part of Vietnam, pro-Chinese
Vietnamese political groups returned in the wake of
Kuomintang troops and tried to abolish all the
political and administrative structures set up by
the Việt Minh. By and by, the Việt Minh administration and its followers withdrew into the shadow of
secrecy.

With the return of the French and the apparent
disappearance of the Việt Minh government, first
from southern Vietnam and over a year later from the
rest of the country, the old divisiveness reestablished itself on the Vietnamese political scene.

The French easily recaptured the support of those who had, not so long before, sided with them. As for those who had gone to the Japanese, they rapidly transferred their allegiance to France. The Việt Minh was left quite alone to struggle against the French reconquest of their old colony, just as they had been left quite alone during the war to resist both the French and the Japanese.

Seen in historical perspective, the Japanese occupation, far from nurturing the nationalist movement of the Vietnamese people, as has so often been presumed, if not said, rather hindered it in two ways. First, by not abolishing French rule in Indochina, the Japanese placed themselves in the position of being competitors to French rule and thereby stimulated French efforts to secure the allegiance of the Indo-chinese populations. French reforms of the civil service designed to recruit and reward Vietnamese bureaucrats and the massive French efforts at mobilizing youth certainly drew some sections of the population closer to them and away from nationalist movements. As a result, the French could afford to deal much more harshly with the nationalists. Next, the Japanese, once they took an active interest in Vietnamese politics, split the nationalist bloc into, roughly speaking, a pro-Japanese and an anti-Japanese

half. Had the Japanese never set foot in Vietnam,
anti-French elements such as the Cao-đài, the Hòa-hảo,
and the Đại Việt might have joined the Việt Minh in
an even grander political coalition and so strengthened the entire nationalist movement. As it was,
the Japanese represented a compromise solution for
these groups. They settled for considerably less
independence than they had hoped for, in return for
a little more power than they had ever had.

In retrospect, it becomes apparent that any
alliance for independence between pro- and anti-
Japanese groups after the war was doomed to failure.
The pro-Japanese factions had been too compromised
politically to play a leading role in the independence struggle and yet they were too suspicious to
accept the control of others. The Việt Minh, on the
other hand, would not tolerate the usual factionalism
and incipient warlordism while they prepared for a
difficult fight against the French. This conflict
led to purges, betrayals, assassinations, execu-
tions--in brief, to the total disruption of the
anti-colonial forces.

While the Japanese sowed division in the nationalist camp, they may, paradoxically enough, have
speeded up the day of independence for Vietnam. The
Japanese military had held up the weakness of the
French forces for all to see, and the lesson was not

lost on the Vietnamese. And if the Japanese did not
promote indigenous government until the very end of
their occupation, still they had allowed the Vietnamese a dizzy taste of self-rule, which they were
not to forget. Acquainted with the vulnerability of
the French and tested in their own strength, the Việt
Minh prepared themselves for an all-out war for independence. Had it not been for the Japanese, other
nationalist groups might have joined these efforts
and remained in the coalition for the duration of
the struggle. Then, too, the present political
cleavages in Vietnam might have been avoided.

NOTES

This article is a revised version of a paper I read at the Regional Meeting of the Association for Asian Studies in August 1969 in San Diego, California. I have greatly benefited from the comments made by Professors Theodore Friend and Grant Goodman. Professors Huỳnh Kim Khánh, David Marr, and Harry Benda made invaluable suggestions. Mr. Trần Văn Chương, although he disagrees with some of my conclusions, nevertheless graciously gave me important insights on a period in which he played an active rôle. It is with gratitude that I acknowledge my indebtedness to all.

[1]See, in John Bastin and Harry J. Benda, *A History of Modern Southeast Asia* (Englewood Cliffs, N. J.: Prentice-Hall, 1968), the chapter titled "The Japanese Interregnum," pp. 123-52.

[2]See Willard H. Elsbree, *Japan's Role in Southeast Asian Nationalist Movements, 1940-1945* (Cambridge, Mass.: Harvard University Press, 1953), pp. 16-17.

[3]Thailand is, of course, not included in the list of Southeast Asian countries in question here for two reasons: Thailand was not a colonial country; and Thailand was an ally of Japan in the war.

[4]General Catroux, *Deux actes du drame indochinois* (Paris, 1959), pp. 60-61.

[5]P. Baudouin, *Neuf mois au gouvernement, avril-décembre 1940* (Paris, 1948), pp. 233, 250.

[6]Baudouin, *Neuf mois*, p. 217: "June 25, 1940: I anounced to the *(Ministers)* Council that, on June 19, Mr. Sumner Welles, Under-Secretary of State, when questioned by our ambassador, Mr. de Saint Quentin, on the American attitude in case of a Japanese aggression against Indochina, replied that the United States would allow it to happen, believing that it was not in their power, in view of the general situation, to enter into a conflict with Japan." P. 248: "July 14, 1940: Mr. Cordell Hull, the Secretary of State, has declared on June 23 to our ambassador in Washington that the entire attention of the United States was turned to Europe, and

266

he advised us to yield to the Japanese demands."
P. 282: "August 7, 1940: The American government
is firmly in favor of a status quo in the Far East--
including in Indochina--but it envisages no practical
measure whatsoever to defend that position." P. 344:
On September 13, 1940, Baudouin was received, in
Paris, by the German ambassador Abetz and the German
counsul general Schleier. Baudouin requested them
to ask Ribbentrop to send a telegram to Tokyo urging
restraint. "It is not," said Baudouin, "in the
interest of the white races to deliver Indochina to
Japanese, Chinese, or Siamese troups." The Germans
answered, "We can but give advice to Tokyo."

[7]Jean Decoux, *A la barre de l'Indochine, Histoire de mon gouvernement général (1940-1945)*
(Paris, 1949), p. 100. The text of the political
agreement is to be found in *International Military
Tribunal for the Far East* (IMTFE), 3 October 1946,
pp. 6936-6939.

[8]Text of the protocol in IMTFE, 3 October 1946,
pp. 6949-6954, and Donald Lancaster, *The Emancipation of French Indochina* (London, 1961), p. 93. For
further details on the Siamese question, see R.
Bauchar, *Rafales sur l'Indochine* (Paris, 1946), pp.
72-88, and Lancaster, *The Emancipation*, pp. 94-96.

[9]Decoux, *A la barre.* Decoux judged that he had
succeeded in that undertaking. On page 104, he
wrote that he was able "during almost five years, to
impose upon 25 million indigenous people as well as
upon the Japanese might which was formidable, the
respect of our sovereignty."

[10]John T. McAlister, Jr., *Viet-Nam: The Origins
of Revolution* (New York: Knopf, 1969), p. 119.

[11]Democratic Republic of Vietnam, *Thirty years
of Struggle of the Party* (Hanoi, 1960), pp. 67-70.

[12]Department of State, OIR Report, No. 3708:
Political Alignments of Vietnamese Nationalists
(Washington, D.C., 1949), p. 44.

[13]According to Paul Mus, *Problèmes de l'Indochine contemporaine; La Formation des partis annamites* (Paris, n.d.), p. 12, the repression was responsible for more than 6,000 arrests and several
dozen executions.

[14]Bauchar, *Rafales sur l'Indochine*, p. 20.

^{15}Philippe Devillers, *Histoire du Vietnam* (Paris, 1952), p. 85.

^{16}Decoux, *A la barre*, p. 393.

^{17}Gouvernement Général de l'Indochine, *Souverains et Notabilités de l'Indochine* (n.p., 1943).

^{18}Trần Huy Liệu and Nguyễn Khắc Đạm, *Xã-hội Việt-Nam trong thời Pháp-Nhật (1939-1945)* (Vietnamese Society Under the French and the Japanese (1939-1945)), 2 vols. (Hanoi, 1957)1:38-43.

^{19}Devillers, *Histoire du Vietnam*, p. 85.

^{20}Maurice Ducoroy, *Ma trahison en Indochine* (Paris, 1949), p. 91.

^{21}Decoux, *A la barre*, p. 204: "...no Japanese interference in, no Japanese control over, the services of the governorship general nor of the Indochinese administration."

^{22}Elsbree, *Japan's Role*, p. 24.

^{23}Democratic Republic of Vietnam, *Thirty Years*, p. 59.

^{24}Ibid., p. 52.

^{25}The latest details in a Western language about Caodaism and its history and philosophy are to be found in Ralph Smith, "An Introduction to Caodaism," in *Bulletin of the School of Oriental and African Studies*, vol. 33, no. 2 (1970), pp. 335-49, and no. 3, pp. 573-89, and Nguyễn Trần Huân, "Histoire d'une sect religieuse au Vietnam," in J. Chesneaux, ed., *Tradition et Révolution au Vietnam* (Paris, 1971), pp. 189-215.

^{26}A. M. Savani, *Visages et images du Sud Vietnam* (Saigon, 1955), p. 78.

^{27}Trần Quang Vinh, *Lịch-sử đạo Cao-đài trong thời-kỳ Phục quốc, 1941-46* (History of the Cao-đài Religion in the Period of National Restoration, 1941-46) (Saigon, 1967), pp. 13-47.

^{28}For more information about the Hòa-hảo, see Savani, *Visages*.

^{29}Trần Quang Vinh, *Lịch-sử đạo Cao-đài*, p. 45.

[30]Trần Trọng Kim has now written his memoirs concerning this period and his rôle in it. They are published under the title *Một cơn gió bụi* (A Lash of Wind and Dust) (Saigon, 1969).

[31]Interview of Professor Huỳnh Kim Khánh with Mr. M. Yokoyama. Mr. Yokoyama arrived in Vietnam in 1941 to be the economic adviser to the Japanese Embassy. Later, he headed a mission of inquiry into the natural resources of Indochina. He was also the president of the Nippo-Franco-Vietnamese Cultural Institute. After March 9, 1945, he was, practically speaking, the Japanese ambassador to the Vietnam government in Huế. I am indebted to Professor Huỳnh Kim Khánh for allowing me to use the text of the interview.

[32]See *Cách-mạng tháng Tám* (The August Revolution) 2 vols., revised by Trần Huy Liệu (Hanoi, 1960).

[33]See Phạm Ngọc Thạch, "Thanh-niên tiên-phong" (The Vanguard Youth), in *Những ngày tháng tám; hồi ký cách-mạng* (The Days in August; Revolutionary Memoirs) (Hanoi, 1961), pp. 238-44.

INDEX

ASIAN STUDIES AT HAWAII

(No. 1) *Bibliography of English Language Sources on Human Ecology, Eastern Malaysia and Brunei.* Compiled by Conrad P. Cotter with the assistance of Shiro Saito. Two Parts. September 1965.

No. 2 *Economic Factors in Southeast Asian Social Change.* Robert Van Niel, editor. May 1968.

No. 3 *East Asian Occasional Papers (1).* Harry J. Lamley, editor. May 1969.

No. 4 *East Asian Occasional Papers (2).* Harry J. Lamley, editor. July 1970.

No. 5 *A Survey of Historical Source Materials in Java and Manila.* Robert Van Niel. February 1971.

No. 6 *Educational Theory in the People's Republic of China.* Commentary and translation by John N. Hawkins. May 1971.

No. 7 *Hai Jui Dismissed from Office.* By Wu Han. Translated by C. C. Huang. May 1972.